TRICKY
LOGIC
PUZZLES
FOR ADULTS

TRICKY
LOGIC
PUZZLES

FOR ADULTS
80+ DIFFICULT PUZZLES TO CHALLENGE YOUR BRAIN

STEVEN CLONTZ

ROCKRIDGE
PRESS

Interior & Cover Designer: Emma Hall
Art Producer: Karen Williams
Editor: Mary Colgan
Production Editor: Matthew Burnett

Cover and interior designed by Creative Giant Inc.,
Mike Thomas, Chris Dickey, Paul Tutrone

ISBN: 978-1-646-11145-9
R0

INTRODUCTION

Perhaps you have seen this classic '80s commercial. A guy is walking down the street, working on a jigsaw puzzle. A woman is walking toward him, engrossed in her algebra textbook. Not paying attention, they bump into each another, scattering the pieces of the puzzle across the pages of the book. They're startled, a little embarrassed. But the accident has a happy ending: They quickly discover that mixing puzzles and logic just makes both things better!

Hmm . . . no, you're right. There's no way I'm remembering that commercial right. I mean, how was that guy solving a jigsaw puzzle while walking down the road? But since you picked up this book, I'm betting you agree that there are few things better than the satisfaction of solving a clever logic puzzle.

As a math educator and researcher, math puzzles are a regular part of my life. What you may not know is that there's not much of a difference between mathematics and logic puzzles! Sure, not every mathematics PhD candidate writes their dissertation on Sudoku puzzles (although I had a buddy in grad school who did). But in both logic puzzles and mathematics, we find ourselves struggling with the information provided, hopefully persevering until we reach that *A-ha!* moment. Clicking that final piece into place is what it's all about.

I've employed that same philosophy in writing this book. I've constructed puzzles in five of the most engaging formats out there: Sudoku, Masyu, Nonograms, Calcudoku, and Logic Grids. Don't worry if any of these are new to you. I'll explain how to play each puzzle type with an introductory warm-up puzzle. As you progress through the book, you'll find the puzzles become increasingly tricky, so you can enjoy building (or refreshing) your skills before tackling the real stumpers.

I've also pulled together puzzles from my favorite genre: Cryptic Puzzles! You'll be breaking codes and thinking creatively to figure out how each conundrum can be solved. But while one cryptic puzzle may seem wildly different from another, there are still tricks you can use, and I've included tips to help you along the way.

While you could work through this book from cover to cover, there's no need to do so. Find your favorite puzzle type or level of difficulty and dive on in! And if you find yourself stuck, I've provided hints and answers if you need them. Puzzles are meant to be fun, so I hope you'll enjoy this book in whatever way suits you. By the way, did you know there's a nonprofit organization that puts together free puzzle meetups on the second Tuesday of every month, located at pubs in more than sixty cities across the world? Check out More Puzzle Fun (page 174) in the back of the book to learn more.

Enjoy!

Steven

HINTS

How to use the hints:

SUDOKU

Each hint describes a full row or column of the grid.

MASYU

Each hint describes the directions of the line as it passes through a black dot, where N is north/up, S is south/down, E is east/right, and W is west/left.

NONOGRAM

Each hint describes a full row or column of the grid. Numbers in parentheses represent the blank cells of the row or column.

CALCUDOKU

Each hint describes a full cage of the grid. Each group of numbers describes a row of the cage.

LOGIC GRID

Each hint is an additional clue.

CRYPTIC PUZZLE

Each hint sheds some light on how to extract the hidden message.

SUDOKU WARM-UP 1

The name "sudoku" is an acronym, coined in the 1980s for a longer Japanese phrase that translates to "the digits must be single." The first sudoku-type puzzles appeared more than 100 years ago in a French newspaper, but sudoku as we know it didn't show up in American puzzle books until the late 1970s.

The rules are simple: Fill in the numbers 1 through 9 within the grid so that each number appears exactly once in each row, column, and 3-by-3 subsquare.

TIPS

⊙ Start by finding a row, column, or subsquare that has only a few blank spaces. Consider which numbers are missing and look at the intersecting rows, columns, and subsquares to see if you can deduce where to place at least one of the numbers.

⊙ In this warm-up puzzle, the second-to-last column is only missing a 1 and a 2. The 2 cannot be placed in the upper blank because a 2 is already present in that row, just to the right of the blank. Therefore, the 2 belongs in the lower blank. By process of elimination, that means the 1 goes in the top blank.

9	7	8	6	2	4	1	5	3
5	3	1	9	8	7	2	6	4
6	4	2	5	1	3	8	9	7
7	8	9	4	6	5	3	1	2
1	2	3	7	9	8	6	4	5
4	5	6	1	3	2	9	7	8
3	6	5	2	4	1	7	8	9
2	1	4	8	7	9	5	3	6
8	9	7	3	5	6	4	2	1

HINT: Column 2: 734 825 619

MASYU | WARM-UP 2

Masyu (pronounced "MA-shoo") is a Japanese word meaning "evil influence." The objective is to draw a loop (consisting of horizontal and vertical lines) that passes through each box that contains a circle. When the line passes through a black circle, it must turn 90 degrees while passing straight through both adjacent squares. The rules for white circles are the opposite. The line must pass straight through white circles but must turn 90 degrees through one or both adjacent squares. The line does not have to pass through every square of the grid. See the example below.

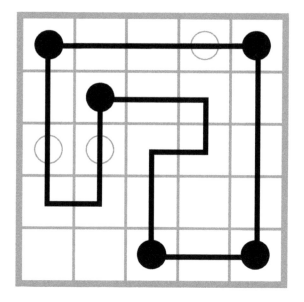

TIPS

> Each white circle on the edge must have a line passing through it parallel to the edge.

> Each black circle on the edge must have a line extending two squares into the grid. The same holds true for black circles one square away from the edge.

HINT: 3rd row, 6th column: SW

NONOGRAM | WARM-UP 3

Unlock Your Potential

Nonogram puzzles are known by a variety of names, including Picross, Paint-By-Number, Griddlers, and Logic Art. Solving (and designing!) these puzzles is a joy because rather than a grid of numbers or symbols, the end result is a pixelated image. Half the fun is figuring out what you're drawing as you solve the puzzle.

Each cell of the grid will be either left blank or filled in. To solve a nonogram, consider the numbers at the boundaries. Each number represents a continuous block of filled-in squares, ordered top to bottom or left to right.

TIPS

⊛ You're told how many cells are filled in for each block, but the puzzle doesn't tell you how far apart each block is! You'll have to logically deduce this yourself.

⊛ If you know a cell must be left blank, mark it with a small dot.

⊛ In this warm-up puzzle, every cell in the first and last columns should be left blank, but every cell in the middle column must be filled in.

⊛ There's also only one way to fill in the second-to-last column: You need two groups of filled-in cells, and they have to be separated by at least one blank cell.

⊛ The title of each puzzle is a clue to what you're drawing.

⊛ In the provided hint for each nonogram, the numbers in parentheses describe blocks of blank cells between the shaded blocks.

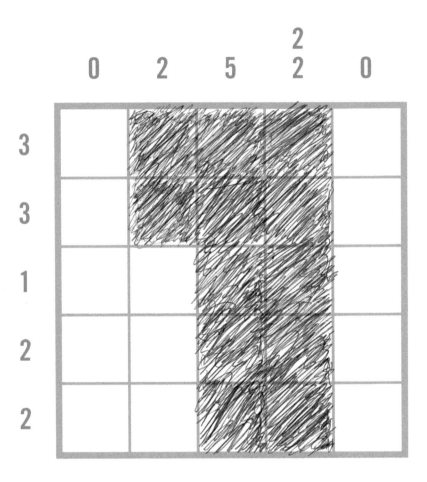

HINT: Column 2: 2(3)

CALCUDOKU WARM-UP 4

You probably won't be surprised to learn that Calcudoku, a variant of sudoku that is also known as KenKen, was created by a mathematics teacher. Tetsuya Miyamoto, an innovator in the art of "Teaching without Teaching," invented the puzzle to motivate his students to practice their skills and logical thinking. Way to go, Mr. Miyamoto!

A Calcudoku puzzle uses the numbers 1 through 4 for a 4-by-4 puzzle, 1 through 5 for a 5-by-5 puzzle, and so on. Like in sudoku, each row and column must contain each number exactly once (creating what mathematicians call a Latin square). But, unlike a sudoku puzzle, none of the numbers are provided. You need to use logic to place the numbers in each cell according to the clues given in each "cage." Addition (+) or multiplication (x) clues describe the sum or product of the caged numbers. Subtraction (–) or division (÷) clues describe the difference or quotient of the larger number by the smaller number in the cage—subtraction and division cages always have two cells. Numbers can be repeated within a cage as long as they don't share a row or column.

TIPS

⊛ Large cages with small rules, such as the three-cell 4+ cage in the lower-right of the following puzzle, don't have many options. The only way to add three numbers 1 through 4 to get a sum of 4 is 1 + 1 + 2. Since the square must be "Latin" like a sudoku puzzle, the 1s must be in different rows and columns, so there's only one possible way to fill the numbers in.

⊛ Cages with multiplication rules can be solved by considering the various factorizations of the number. For example, the rule 24x factors into the prime numbers 2 x 2 x 2 x 3. Since the cage has only three cells, two of those numbers must be combined; since the numbers must be 1 through 4, the only possibility is 2 x 3 x 4. The number 1 could be used as well, except that two more numbers would need to be combined—for example, 1 x 4 x 6 or 1 x 3 x 8, and 6 and 8 are not allowed in this puzzle.

HINT: 24x cage: 23 4

11

LOGIC GRID | WARM-UP 5

Logic grid puzzles are perhaps the purest type of logic puzzle, since no explanation of the mechanics is necessary. All you have to do is use logic to figure out the relationships between the various people or items being discussed.

But don't let that fool you into thinking they are easy! That's where the grid comes into play. Using it, you can make notes on the relationships between each pair of properties, ruling out the impossible until only the possible remains.

Logic grid puzzles are often known as "zebra" puzzles, as a puzzle very similar to the final logic grid puzzle in this book first appeared in *Life International* magazine in 1963, asking the solver to identify the owner of the zebra. Although it won't help you solve the following clues, it's worth noting that some people also refer to logic grid puzzles as "Einstein riddles," as such puzzles are often misattributed to the famous physicist Albert Einstein. Legend has it that a young Albert first invented the original zebra puzzle as a child, but as it's also been credited to Lewis Carroll (author of *Alice's Adventures in Wonderland*), I'd take such rumors with a grain of salt.

TIPS

⊙ Read each clue carefully in order. If a clue prevents a relationship, mark the appropriate location in the grid with an X. If only one cell in a row or column remains, that must be the correct relationship—mark it with an O!

⊙ If a clue directly asserts a relationship, mark the appropriate location in the grid with an O, and then mark every other relationship in its row and column with an X.

⊙ You may need to revisit old clues after more information has been revealed from later clues.

Make Yourself at Home

For our first puzzle, we have four houses lined up on a street, where the first house is on the far left and the last house is on the far right. Using the following clues, can you determine which house is which color (blue, green, ivory, or yellow) and who owns which house (Alice, Bob, Carl, or Diana)?

CLUES:

⊙ Carl lives in the first (leftmost) house.

⊙ Neither Alice nor Diana lives in the blue house.

⊙ Diana lives to the left of the ivory house and next to the green house.

⊙ Bob lives next to the blue house.

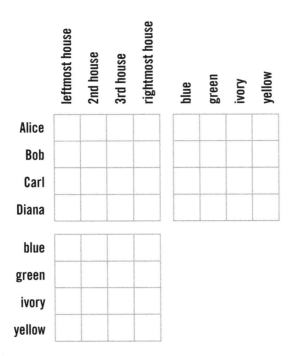

HINT: Alice lives in the rightmost house.

CRYPTIC PUZZLE | WARM-UP 6

While I've been solving puzzles like sudoku for a long time, I didn't consider myself a puzzle enthusiast until I played in my first puzzle hunt. In a puzzle hunt, each team is presented with several challenges, each of which decodes a hidden word or phrase. In some hunts, the solutions will even lead you to locations spread across an entire city.

Usually the hunt has a theme or a plot, so if you've ever fantasized about finding a map on the back of the Declaration of Independence or cracking a code written by Leonardo da Vinci, these events are probably for you! I've been playing and designing such hunts for more than a decade, but in recent years, a wider audience has been able to enjoy similar experiences on a smaller scale: escape rooms. In the back of the book, I recommend a few ways to get into these sorts of events, no matter where you live.

The challenges found in puzzle hunts or escape rooms are often simply called "puzzles," but to distinguish them from other types of puzzles in this book, I'll call them "cryptic puzzles." Cryptic puzzles may be based on logic, trivia, or wordplay, but for this book, I'm focusing on logic-based challenges.

TIPS

⊛ There are two distinguishing characteristics of cryptic puzzles. First, each puzzle solves to a short word or phrase; second, the cryptic method of extracting this hidden message changes from puzzle to puzzle, and it's up to you to figure it out!

⊛ I've based many of these cryptic puzzles on the other five puzzle types found in this book, so those puzzle-solving skills should help you here as well.

⊛ Once the first layer of the puzzle has been solved, you'll need to think creatively about how I might have hidden the solution until you reach that epiphany or *A-ha!* moment. I've provided blanks to fill in your answer when you find it; if it doesn't fit, keep thinking!

⊛ You can check your answers in the back of the book, or you can check your own work by seeing if your answers fit together in the "metapuzzle." Flip to the Cryptic Puzzle on page 160 to see what I'm talking about.

Getting Started

8	9	I	6	2	5			
	5		8		7	9	6	2
7		2	1	G	3	N		4
2	3	1	5	N			9	
9	8	I	3		2	4		5
6						E	3	8
4	7	6	9	5		1		G
3	2	8		7		6		
	B	9	2	3	N		4	

☐ ☐ ☐ ☐ ☐ ☐ ☐ ☐ ☐

Answer on page 162

HINT: By solving the sudoku puzzle like normal, you should be able to unscramble the letters IGNNIEGBN found in the grid.

15

SUDOKU 7

See directions on page 4

TIP

⊙ If you can't figure out exactly where to place a number, you can write all the possibilities as small numbers at the top of each cell. This will make it easier to consider each possibility and rule out the possibilities that would result in logical contradictions.

1		2	6					9
7	9					4		
4			9	8		1		3
3	5	6						
				1			6	5
	4		5	6	3	8		
		3	2	4	6		7	
	2			7		5	3	1
9	8	7						2

HINT: Row 8: 624 879 531

MASYU

See directions on page 6

TIPS

▶ If you can deduce that a cell's edge cannot be passed through, mark it with a small X so you remember this later. In harder puzzles, lines will be drawn only because there will be no other options left.

▶ Don't forget that you want to produce a single loop. A solution that creates a loop that doesn't pass through all circles is invalid. This will also help you mark square edges that shouldn't be passed through.

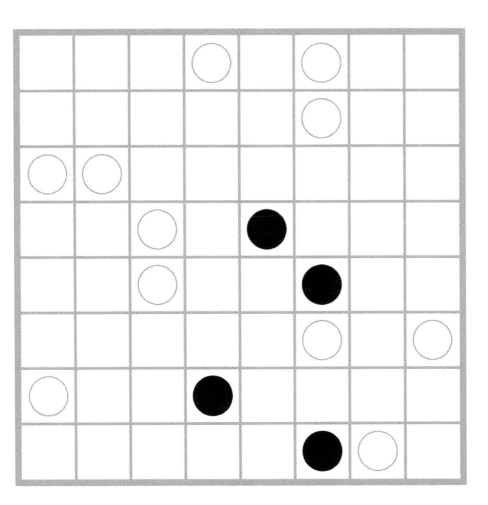

HINT: 4th row, 5th column: NE **17**

NONOGRAM  9

See directions on page 8

Ruffing It

TIPS

❯ Look for large numbers first. There are only two possibilities to complete the columns marked with a 9, so go ahead and fill in the middle 8 cells that would be filled in either way.

❯ The same idea works for the rows marked with 6 and 8.

❯ Think about all the possible ways the 4 can fit into each 4, 2 column. Shade the cell that will be filled in every scenario.

❯ Don't forget: Each block of filled-in cells can be separated by one, two, or more blank cells.

			1 2	4	4	1 2			
1	3	9	2	2	2	2	9	3	1

3 3										
2 2										
8										
1 2 1										
1 2 1										
6										
2 2										
1 1										
6										
4										

HINT: Row 4: (2)1(1)2(1)1(2)

CALCUDOKU  10

See directions on page 10

TIPS

⊙ Every number ending with 0 or 5 is a multiple of 5, so finding multiplication cages that require a 5 is easy.

⊙ In this particular puzzle, the 15x cage with three cells must contain a 1, a 3, and a 5. The 20x cage with two cells will contain a 4 and a 5. This means the middle cell in the 15x cage cannot contain a 5.

7+		**2-**	**2-**	
5+	**20x**		**13+**	
		3÷		**3-**
3-				
15x			**2-**	

HINT: 13+ cage: 4 1 3 5

19

LOGIC GRID  11

See directions on page 12

No Reservations

TIP

- Don't forget that a clue that states that two items are back-to-back, before, or after each other means that they cannot be the same item. Go ahead and mark that relationship with an X; You can use the rest of the clue later once you've filled out the grid more.

Five friends (Alvin, Bart, Carol, Doug, and Erin) have agreed to meet up for dinner. Can you deduce in what order they arrived at the restaurant as well as determine their hobbies (band, cooking, hiking, karaoke, or photography)?

CLUES:

- Erin, who arrived after the cooking enthusiast, doesn't like to hike.
- The hiking fan and Alvin arrived back-to-back.
- The karaoke fan arrived third.
- Doug arrived before Carol, who likes to cook.
- The photographer and Erin arrived back-to-back.

	first	second	third	fourth	last		band	cooking	hiking	karaoke	photography
Alvin											
Bart											
Carol											
Doug											
Erin											
band											
cooking											
hiking											
karaoke											
photography											

Answer on page 162

HINT: Bart arrived last.

CRYPTIC PUZZLE 12

See directions on page 14

We're Number One!

TIP

⊙ The title of a cryptic puzzle is often related to either the method of solving the puzzle or the puzzle's solution.

3-	3÷	15x	40x	
				1-
3-		12x		
2-			5÷	1-
30x				

☐ ☐ ☐ ☐ ☐

HINT: The title of the puzzle is a clue to use the 1s in the solved Calcudoku to unscramble the letters OCTUN.

See directions on page 4

	4			9				2
2				6	4	7		8
	7	9			1		6	5
6					8		4	
9	8			4	2			
	2			5			7	9
		2	7		9	5	1	
		8	3			6		
3	5	1		2		9		

HINT: Column 8: 396 457 128

See directions on page 6

HINT: 6th row, 5th column: NW

23

NONOGRAM 15

Stay Dry

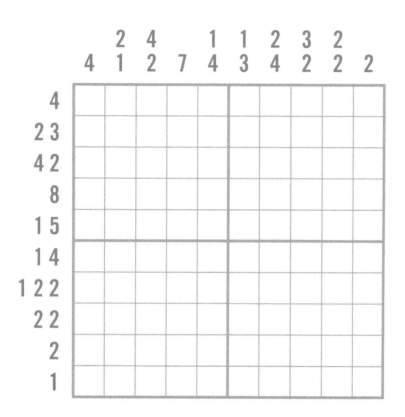

See directions on page 8

Column clues:
2 4 · 1 1 2 3 2
4 1 2 7 4 3 4 2 2 2

Row clues:
4
2 3
4 2
8
1 5
1 4
1 2 2
2 2
2
1

See directions on page 10

3-		**30x**		
6x	**30x**		**2÷**	**4÷**
	20x			
		3x		**15x**
40x				

See directions on page 14

Follow the Path

HINT: The title suggests following the path given by the solved Masyu puzzle, observing the arrow on the left side of the puzzle.

LOGIC GRID  18

See directions on page 12

Ready, Set, Go!

Aiden, Beth, Chloe, Diego, and Everett have decided to participate in a pentathlon, which involves archery, biking, fencing, footracing, and swimming. Each person specializes in a particular sport out of those five. Can you figure out each person's speciality and in which place they finished the competition?

CLUES:

⊚ The archery specialist and Chloe placed next to each other.

⊚ Aiden did better than the biking enthusiast but worse than the fencing expert.

⊚ Chloe did better than the swimming and archery experts.

⊚ The natural swimmer and Everett placed back-to-back.

⊚ The biking fan finished third.

⊚ Beth is the best fencer of the group.

	1st place	2nd place	3rd place	4th place	5th place	archery	biking	fencing	footracing	swimming
Aiden										
Beth										
Chloe										
Diego										
Everett										
archery										
biking										
fencing										
footracing										
swimming										

Answer on page 163

HINT: Diego finished last.

See directions on page 4

3	6	5	2				7	
8			3		6	1	4	
				7	9		5	3
1				9		5		
4	5	6				8		7
7			4	6		2		
	7		6	2	4			5
		2		1	3	7		9
5	3				7		2	6

NONOGRAM 21

The Best Offense

See directions on page 8

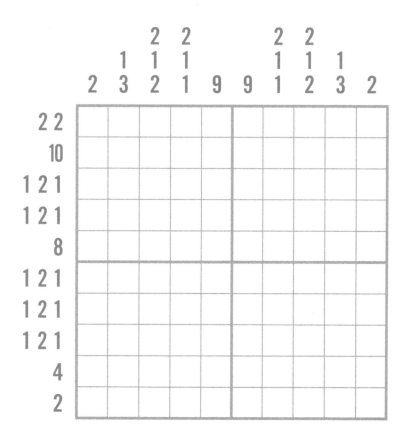

HINT: Column 3: 2(2)1(1)2(2)   Picture Description: Shield

CALCUDOKU 22

See directions on page 10

3-		8+	3-	
15x				1-
120x				
12x	2÷		8+	
			7+	

HINT: 12x cage: 1 3 1 4

31

LOGIC GRID 23

See directions on page 12

Tune In

A television studio is piloting five new shows, which conveniently have been given working titles based on the first five letters in the phonetic alphabet: Alpha, Bravo, Charlie, Delta, and Echo. Can you determine the genre of each show (comedy, drama, game show, news, or talk show) as well as their relative ratings?

CLUES:

- Charlie received the second-worst ratings.
- Echo did worse than the talk show, which did worse than Delta.
- Bravo is a news show.
- Echo isn't a comedy, and it did better than the game show.

	best	2nd	3rd	4th	worst	comedy	drama	game show	news	talk show
Alpha										
Bravo										
Charlie										
Delta										
Echo										
comedy										
drama										
game show										
news										
talk show										

Answer on page 163

HINT: Alpha received the second-best ratings.

CRYPTIC PUZZLE 24

See directions on page 14

Initial Here

CLUES:

- Ronald stands next to Crystal.
- Yousef stands to the left of Mary.
- Oliver stands by Ronald and Nick.
- Crystal stands to the right of Andrew.
- Yousef stands next to Nick.
- Nick stands to the right of Oliver.

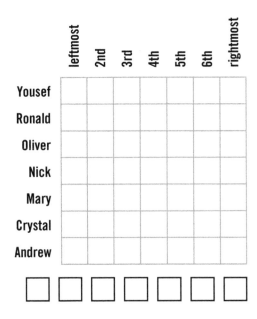

HINT: The title of the puzzle is a clue to use the first letter of each name, once you've ordered them from left to right according to the logic grid puzzle.

33

SUDOKU 25

See directions on page 4

3		5				2		6
			1	5			7	
7			2			1		5
	3			7		6	5	
	9	7		4	5			
	6					9	8	7
		3	4		1			
9	7	8			6			2
		2		8	9	5	6	

HINT: Column 5: 956 741 238

See directions on page 6

HINT: 3rd row, 1st column: NE

35

NONOGRAM  27

For Your Flowers

See directions on page 8

```
                    2
                    1  1              1  2
              1  1  2  1  1  2  1  1
              1  1  1  2  1  2  1  1
           5  1  1  1  1  1  1  1  2  5
        8
      1 1
      1 1
      3 3
      1 1
1 1 1 1 1
  1 2 2 1
  1 1 1 1
      1 2
        8
```

Answer on page 164   Picture Description: Vase   HINT: Row 6: 1(1)1(1)1(1)1(2)1

CALCUDOKU 28

See directions on page 10

5÷		18x		1-
8+	2-			
	50x			6x
	3-			
1-		20x		

HINT: 50x cage: 5 2 1 5

CRYPTIC PUZZLE 29

See directions on page 14

Capitalization Is Key

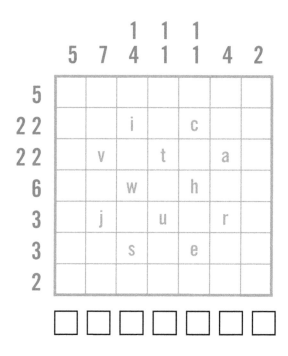

 Answer on page 164 HINT: Some of the lowercase letters in the grid will be used, but the title suggests that a capital letter must also be used.

See directions on page 4

5	6	4					7	
2				9		5		
			5	6		2	1	
		5	7			4	6	2
	8		4		6		5	1
	2	6	3		5			8
9				5	3	1		
1	4	2			8			
					2	9	8	7

HINT: Row 9: 653 142 987

See directions on page 6

HINT: 4th row, 6th column: NE

Setting Up Camp

See directions on page 8

```
                1
      3 2 1 3 2 1 1 2
    5 1 1 7 1 1 5 1 1 4
  5
1 1 1
2 1 1
1 1 1 1
1 1 1 1
1 1 1 1
1 1 1 1
1 1 1 1
1 1 2
  7
```

HINT: Column 8: 1(7)1(1)   Picture Description: Tent

CALCUDOKU 33

See directions on page 10

9+		32x	3-	
15x				3-
	8x	6x		
2÷			11+	
		4-		

HINT: 32x cage: 4 12 4

LOGIC GRID  34

See directions on page 12

The Office

Anna, Beth, Chris, Dean, and Emily all work for the same company. Each has an office on a different floor of a five-story building, and each works for a different department (accounting, human resources [HR], information technology [IT], marketing, or supply chain management).

CLUES:

> Beth's office is just above or below accounting's floor.

> Anna is on the fourth floor.

> Emily's office is just above or below human resources.

> Marketing is above Anna's office.

> Chris works in human resources.

> Anna works in supply chain management.

> Beth's office is above human resources.

	1st floor	2nd floor	3rd floor	4th floor	5th floor	accounting	HR	IT	marketing	supply chain
Anna										
Beth										
Chris										
Dean										
Emily										
accounting					
HR					
IT					
marketing					
supply chain					

HINT: Emily works on the second floor.

See directions on page 14

Diagonalized Anxiety

	I			A		N		
		A			L	M		E
L	M		I					
	S	L		M	U		N	I
			L		T	A	E	
	T			E				S
I	L	T	U				M	
M						A	I		N
S	A	N	E	I		U	L	

☐ ☐ ☐ ☐ ☐ ☐ ☐ ☐ ☐

HINT: Considering the title, "anxiety" refers to the solution, and "diagonalization" refers to how to find the solution.

See directions on page 4

9		7	2			5		
	2		5	6	4	8		
		4	8			2	3	
7	9				2		5	3
5	6			7	8		4	
4			6		3		7	
1	3	5				7		9
			3	1	5			6
		6		8		3		

See directions on page 6

HINT: 6th row, 2nd column: NE

NONOGRAM 38

See directions on page 8

P Is for Puzzle, C Is for. . .

```
                    1   1   1
                2   1   1   1   1   1   2
            1   1   1   2   1   1   2   1
        5   2   2   1   2   1   1   2   2   6
      1
    1 1
  1 1 3
1 3 1 1
1 1 1 2
1 1 1 1
1 1 2 1
2 1 1 2
  2 1 2
      6
```

HINT: Row 4: 1(1)3(1)1(2)1   Picture Description: Cookie   **47**

CRYPTIC PUZZLE 39

See directions on page 14

Untouched

I	M	M	H	◯	M	E	J
R	E	A	Q	◯	U	●	J
◯	N	◯	K	◯	K	P	L
Z	C	O	M	U	R	G	R
●	E	H	Y	●	I	●	B
E	H	C	●	F	L	◯	P
◯	A	T	A	J	F	W	◯
M	Z	◯	R	E	P	O	●

☐ ☐ ☐ ☐ ☐ ☐ ☐ ☐ ☐ ☐

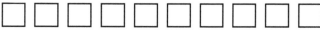

HINT: The title of the puzzle is a clue to use the letters in the squares that are not passed through by the Masyu solution.

LOGIC GRID  40

See directions on page 12

School Is in Session

Adam, Bianca, Cindy, David, and Eric just got their grades back; as you might expect, each student received a different grade from A to F. Can you figure out how they did and what their favorite subjects are?

CLUES:

- Adam did worse than the student whose favorite subject is history.
- Eric and Bianca received almost the same grade as the student who prefers science.
- Cindy did worse than the science enthusiast.
- Adam received a B.
- Bianca received almost the same grade as the math whiz.
- Adam and David earned grades just above or below the student who likes English class best.

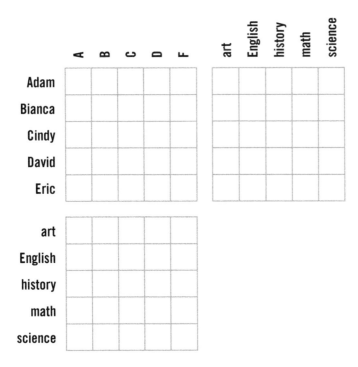

HINT: David earned a D.   **49**

MASYU 41

See directions on page 6

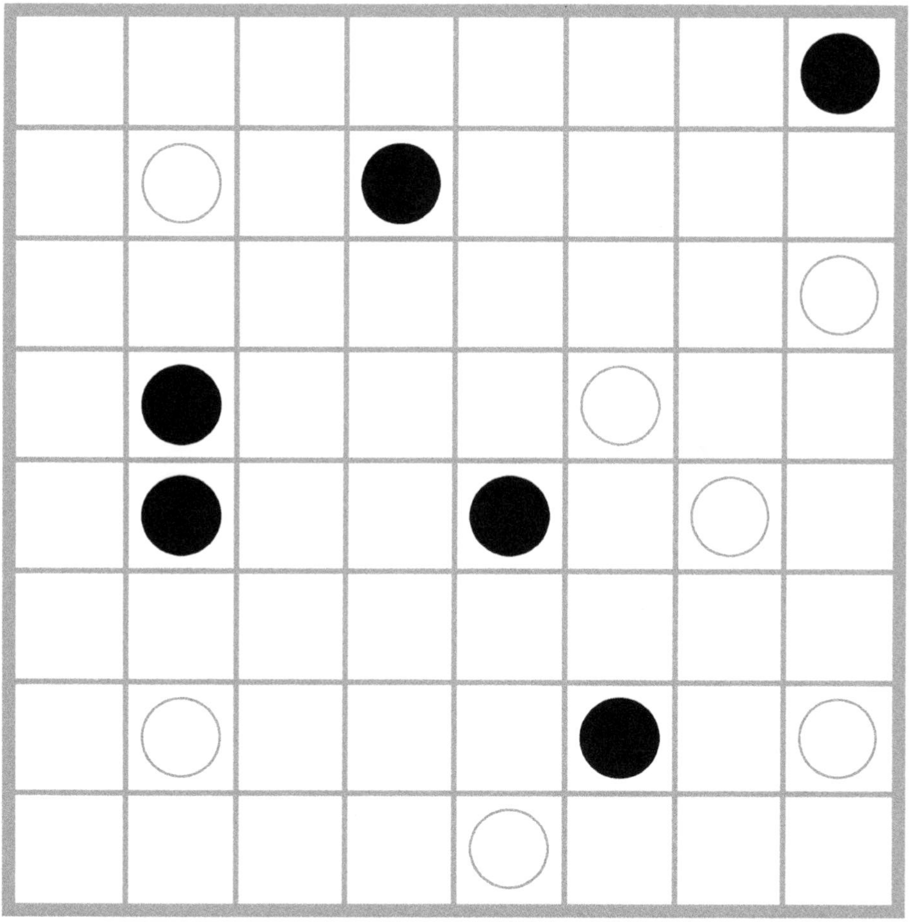

 Answer on page 165

HINT: 5th row, 5th column: NW

NONOGRAM 42

Off the Shelf

Column clues:
```
                1
                1  1  1
                1  1  2        2
          1  1  1  1  1  8  2  1
       9  3  1  3  1  3  1  2  5  3
```

Row clues:
```
       7
     1 2
   1 2 4
   1 1 1
   1 1 4
   1 3 3
   1 1 1
     7 1
 2 1 1 2
       7
```

HINT: Row 7: 1(5)1(1)1(1) Picture Description: Book

See directions on page 10

3÷	2÷	5÷		3-
		12x		
5÷		5+		8+
2-	5÷		10x	
	12x			

HINT: 8+ cage: 4 3 1

LOGIC GRID  44

See directions on page 12

Arr You Ready?

Five fearsome pirates (Arsonnose, Blackbeard, Cursechin, Darkeye, and Evilear) have divvied up buried treasure amounting to 1500 gold coins. Aside from their unique names, each pirate also has a distinguishing feature: a cutlass, eyepatch, hook hand, parrot, or treasure map. How much gold did each pirate receive?

CLUES:

▷ Evilear received about as much gold as the pirate with an eyepatch and more gold than the pirate with a hook for a hand.

▷ The parrot's owner received more gold than Cursechin and almost as much gold as Arsonnose.

▷ Blackbeard received about as much gold as the eyepatch and hook hand pirates.

▷ The owner of the cutlass received 400 gold coins.

	100 gold	200 gold	300 gold	400 gold	500 gold	cutlass	eyepatch	hook hand	parrot	treasure map
Arsonnose										
Blackbeard										
Cursechin										
Darkeye										
Evilear										
cutlass					
eyepatch					
hook hand					
parrot					
treasure map					

HINT: Darkeye received 500 gold coins.

CRYPTIC PUZZLE 45

See directions on page 14

Classical Logic

CLUES:

- $E > \delta$
- $E < \alpha$
- $E \neq \gamma$
- $E > A$
- $C = \gamma \pm 1$
- $\gamma > C$
- $A \neq \alpha$
- $\alpha = D \pm 1$
- $A = \epsilon \pm 1$
- $\beta = 2$

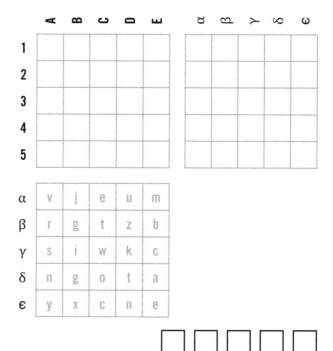

	A	B	C	D	E		α	β	γ	δ	ε
1											
2											
3											
4											
5											

α	v	j	e	u	m
β	r	g	t	z	b
γ	s	i	w	k	c
δ	n	g	o	t	a
ε	y	x	c	n	e

☐ ☐ ☐ ☐ ☐

HINT: Once the logic puzzle is solved, use the lowercase letters that match valid relationships between the English and non-English letters.

	9	8		3		5		
	6				7	2	1	
	3				4	8	7	
8					2	6		
3		6	9					4
2			6	5			8	
6				8			5	1
5			4		6			8
		7					6	

Classic T

See directions on page 8

	3	1 1	1 2 5	1	2 1	2 1	1 2 2	2 5	1 1	2
2 2										
1 3 2										
1 1										
1 2 1 1										
1 1 2 1										
3 2										
1 1										
1 1										
1 2										
5										

HINT: Column 3: 1(2)1(1)5   Picture Description: Shirt

CALCUDOKU 48

See directions on page 10

3÷	12+			2-
	8+			
1-		7+	7+	8+
10x	3-			
			3÷	

HINT: 12+ cage: 534

57

CRYPTIC PUZZLE 49

See directions on page 14

An Amazing Image

Column clues:
```
                              1
            1        1  1     1
            1  3     1  1     1
         1  3  1  3  1  1  1
      9  1  1  1  1  1  1  1  9
```

Row clues and grid:

Clue									
7 1		m			q			l	
1 1 1		g				u			n
1 5 1	r				h			a	
1 1	z			o		b			
1 3 3		x		d					l
1 1 1 1		v	c				y		
3 3 1	k							r	f
1 1		t			n		i		
1 7	e	h				w			

☐ ☐ ☐ ☐ ☐ ☐ ☐ ☐ ☐

HINT: As the title says, the solution to the nonogram is "amazing," that is, a "maze."

LOGIC GRID 50

See directions on page 12

You Can Go Home Again After All

Eve has just moved into the neighborhood with Alice, Bob, Carl, and Diana. To be good neighbors, they let her choose her favorite house and everyone else moved around to accommodate. There are now five houses, which have been repainted five different colors. I know it sounds confusing, but the following clues should help you make sense of where everyone ended up.

CLUES:

⊙ Alice lives in the red house.

⊙ Carl's house is to the right of the green house, which is to the right of Eve's house.

⊙ Diana's house (which is yellow) is next to the blue house.

⊙ Eve moved into the middle house.

	leftmost house	2nd house	middle house	4th house	rightmost house		blue	green	ivory	red	yellow
Alice											
Bob											
Carl											
Diana											
Eve											
blue											
green											
ivory											
red											
yellow											

HINT: Bob lives in the fourth house from the left.

See directions on page 4

	1	3	2		6	8		
			1	3	5	2	4	6
		4					3	5
7	9						5	
4				8				1
			6	5			8	7
		1	5	6		7		8
	7			1	2			
3		6	7			4	1	

See directions on page 6

HINT: 8th row, 3rd column: SW

See directions on page 10

16+		20x		8+	
		5-	4-		
8x			5÷		180x
	2-		9+	2÷	
3-	10+				
			2-		

CRYPTIC PUZZLE 54

See directions on page 14

SUM-ptuous

TIP

⊙ To solve harder cryptic puzzles, you will need to apply various codes. This includes encryptions as simple as A = 1, B = 2, etc., as used in the following puzzle, but more elaborate codes like Morse and Braille may be found in the Code Sheet for Cryptic Puzzles section on page 161.

1	39+			11+
32+	4	19+		
	23+	7	19+	
18+			14	
		15+		18

☐ ☐ ☐ ☐ ☐

HINT: This Calcudoku must be solved using the numbers 1, 4, 7, 14, and 18, each of which corresponds to a different letter of the alphabet.

LOGIC GRID  55

See directions on page 12

Dine and Dash?

Alvin and friends are meeting up for dinner again. Each person just bought a new pair of sneakers. As luck would have it, each pair is in a different color. Since no one can stick to a schedule, it's up to you to figure out when they arrived and who owns which shoes. (And their tastes in hobbies may have changed since last time.)

CLUES:

> The owner of the green shoes arrived just before or after the cooking enthusiast.

> Alvin arrived second.

> The person wearing purple shoes (who dislikes hiking) arrived after Erin.

> Carol isn't too crazy about karaoke.

> The photographer, who arrived first, wears green shoes.

> Doug is proud of his new white shoes.

> Bart arrived immediately before or after the owner of the blue shoes.

> The person wearing purple shoes arrived just between the cooking and karaoke hobbyists.

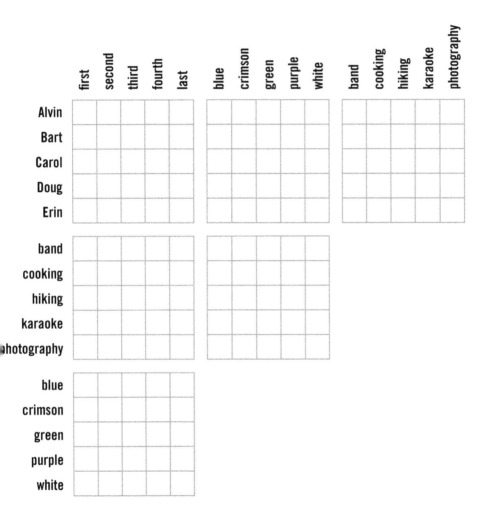

	first	second	third	fourth	last	blue	crimson	green	purple	white	band	cooking	hiking	karaoke	photography
Alvin															
Bart															
Carol															
Doug															
Erin															
band															
cooking															
hiking															
karaoke															
photography															
blue															
crimson															
green															
purple															
white															

			2		6	7		
8	9					4		
			8	7				5
3				5	4		9	
		5					3	
		8			1		6	
	8		4	1				
	3		7				4	
4	2					9	7	8

HINT: Column 4: 218 693 475

See directions on page 6

See directions on page 8

Leaf It to Me

Column clues:

```
1                   1 3       1 1 1 1
1 3 1 1 2 2 1 1 1 2 1
1 3 1 1 2 1 1 2 1 1 1 2
4 1 2 1 3 1 1 1 5 1 1 3 1
4 2 1 3 4 1 1 1 1 2 2 2 1 1 5
```

Row clues:

```
        3 3 2
      3 2 1 1
1 1 1 1 1 2
2 1 1 1 2 1
2 1 1 1 1 2
1 2 1 1 1 1
1 2 1 1 2 1
  2 1 2 1 1
    1 4 2 2
      3 4 2
        1 1
      1 2 2
        1 1
    1 3 1 1
      2 1 2
```

HINT: Row 4: (1)2(1)1(1)1(1)1(1)2(2)1   Picture Description: Tree

CRYPTIC PUZZLE 59

See directions on page 14

To solve, see Code Sheet for Cryptic Puzzles on page 161.

Samuel's Long Odds

7		9	6			3		
			7	1		5		2
				4	8			
	8	4		3		7		
		2	4		6		9	
				7			6	
			6	3				9
4			2	5			3	8
3	6							

☐ ☐ ☐ ☐ ☐ ☐

HINT: The "odd" numbers in the shaded regions represent "long" dashes in a certain code attributed to Samuel M.

LOGIC GRID  60

Rematch

Aiden and his friends decided to have another pentathlon race due to accusations of mistaken identity. To prevent this from happening, they've each agreed to wear a distinctively colored shirt. They've been training, so their specialty event may have changed since the last race, but I'm sure you'll have no trouble sorting it all out.

CLUES:

⊛ Everett and the owner of the black shirt finished back-to-back.

⊛ Chloe is the best foot racer.

⊛ Aiden refuses to wear gray.

⊛ The wearer of the cyan shirt finished just between the footracing expert and Everett.

⊛ The owner of the black shirt finished in first overall, probably due to their finesse in archery.

⊛ Aiden isn't a great fencer.

⊛ Diego didn't wear the black shirt.

⊛ The best biker finished back-to-back with Diego.

⊛ Chloe wore a red shirt.

⊛ Aiden finished after the best archer.

	1st place	2nd place	3rd place	4th place	5th place	black	cyan	gray	pink	red	archery	biking	fencing	footracing	swimming
Aiden															
Beth															
Chloe															
Diego															
Everett															
archery															
biking															
fencing															
footracing															
swimming															
black															
cyan															
gray															
pink															
red															

HINT: Beth finished first.

See directions on page 6

HINT: 6th row, 6th column: SW

NONOGRAM 62

Less Than Three

See directions on page 8

```
                              1
              2 1 5           2 2
          3 3 3 1 6     1     5 1 2 3 9 9
          5 2 3 2 1 7 7 7 6 1 2 3 5 3 2
          2 1 2 1 2 4 3 4 5 3 2 1 3 1 2
      3 1 5
        2 4
    1 3 3 3
        9 2
        9 2
        8 3
      1 7 3
      2 5 4
      3 3 5
      4 1 1 1
1 1 1 1 2 2
  1 1 1 2 5
      3 5 3
  1 1 7 1 1
      2 9 2
```

HINT: Column 11: 2(5)2(1)3(1)1 Picture Description: Hearts **73**

See directions on page 10

8+			2-		24x
2-	4-	1-		90x	
11+	1-	1-	24x		5-
				12+	
12x		1-			

HINT: Lower 24x cage: 42 3

CRYPTIC PUZZLE 64

See directions on page 14

To solve, see Code Sheet for Cryptic Puzzles on page 161.

Some Puzzle

CLUES:

⊗ Babe isn't interested in words beginning with B.

⊗ Porky prefers cartoons.

⊗ Wilbur's best friend is a spider.

⊗ Cartoons and blue don't go together; neither do Porky and red.

HINT: Babe, Porky, and Wilbur are famous examples of a certain animal, related to a certain code.

LOGIC GRID  65

Don't Touch That Dial

Development of the five new television shows is progressing smoothly. As such, the studio will pilot each of the five shows on a different public access channel to get a better measure of their ratings. Each of the shows has been retooled, so their genres may be different than the previous puzzle, but maybe that helped the ratings of a few.

CLUES:

⊙ Charlie, a comedy, performed just slightly worse than the show aired on WULV.

⊙ Bravo, which was aired on WQKG, earned the second-best ratings.

⊙ The game show had the worst ratings of all.

⊙ Echo did better than the show on WSBA.

⊙ Delta isn't a drama, and it performed almost as well as the news show.

⊙ The show on WRDE did about as well as the talk show.

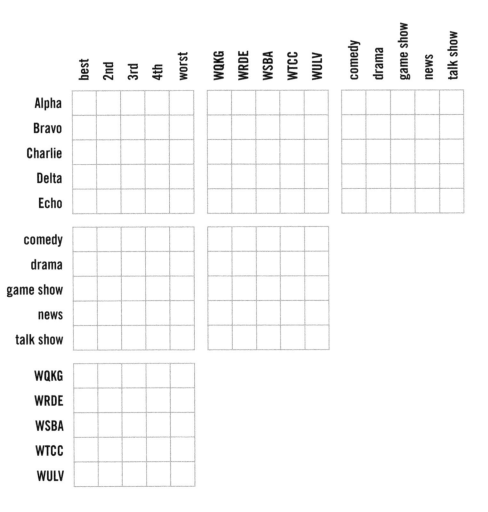

HINT: Alpha received the worst ratings.

See directions on page 4

			4			8	9	
2		1	7					
	7	9					1	
	6		3	2		7	8	
1						4		6
7	9	8		5				
	1			7	9			2
		4	1					8
	8				6	5	3	

HINT: Column 3: 619 528 347

See directions on page 6

HINT: 4th row, 5th column: SW

NONOGRAM 68

Has a Cold Shoulder

See directions on page 8

```
                    1           1           3                   1
                    1  1  2  1     1     2                      1
                    2  1  1  2     1     1  3  4        1        2
                    1  2  1  1  1  4  2  1  1  1     7  1  1  1
                    1  2  1  2  1  1  2  1  1  1  4  2  1  2  1
                    1  1  3  1  2  2  2  2  2  2  3  1  4  1  1
     1 1 2 5 1
           2 5
             1 9
       1 2 1 3 1
       1 1 1 1 1
   1 2 1 1 1 1 2
       2 1 1 1 1
       1 1 2 1 1
       1 1 1 1 2
         1 1 6 1
             1 1 1
       1 2 3 2 1
         1 2 2 1
         2 3 1 1
         1 2 3 2
```

HINT: Row 8: (1)(3)(1)(2)(1)(1)(2)

See directions on page 10

10+			14+	2÷	
120x		1-		12+	
9+					
	18x	11+		4-	
			5-		12x
2÷		120x			

HINT: 12+ cage: 31 26

CRYPTIC PUZZLE 70

See directions on page 14

To solve, see Code Sheet for Cryptic Puzzles on page 161.

Feeling Fine

1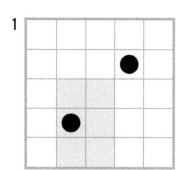

2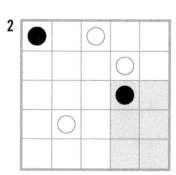

3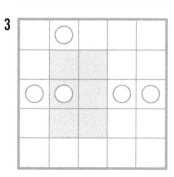

4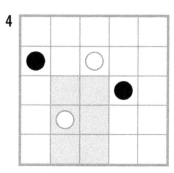

5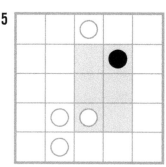

☐ ☐ ☐ ☐ ☐

HINT: A certain code uses 3X2 rectangles shaded in each square; it also is related to the word "Feeling."

See directions on page 4

						7	8	
9		8	1			5		
6		3	9	7	8			
	8		3		5			4
			4		6	8	9	7
	2						5	
				9			1	
				3		6	4	5
2	3	1		6				

HINT: Row 9: 231 564 978 **83**

CALCUDOKU 73

See directions on page 10

5+	180x	4-		11+	1-
30x	1-		4+		1-
	1-			3÷	
4÷	60x				540x
	2÷				

HINT: 540x cage: 6 653

85

Office Space

Management has just increased security at the office, assigning Anna and her colleagues a security level of A through E. They've also reassigned employees to various departments and moved around offices to boot. Given this level of corporate shakeup, perhaps it's time that they brush up their résumés. In the meantime, you can find their new office locations by considering the following clues.

CLUES:

- Accounting is located on the second floor.
- Marketing is located above the floor with security level D.
- Security level C is located below the accounting department.
- Beth is below the floor requiring security level B.
- Security level D is just above or below Beth's floor.
- Anna works in human resources.
- Beth, who has security level E, has an office above Chris.
- Chris is just below the supply chain management floor.
- Emily is on the second floor.

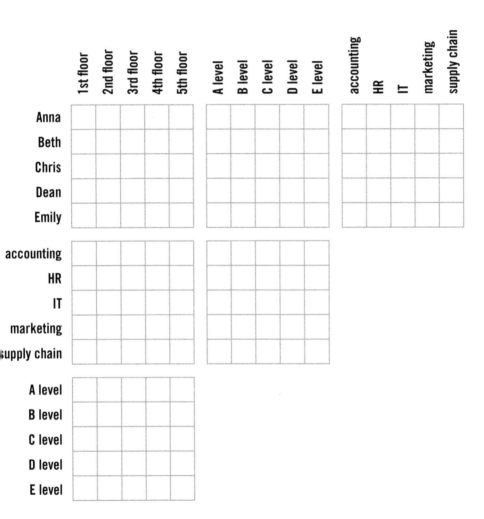

CRYPTIC PUZZLE 75

See directions on page 14

Rebus's Makeup

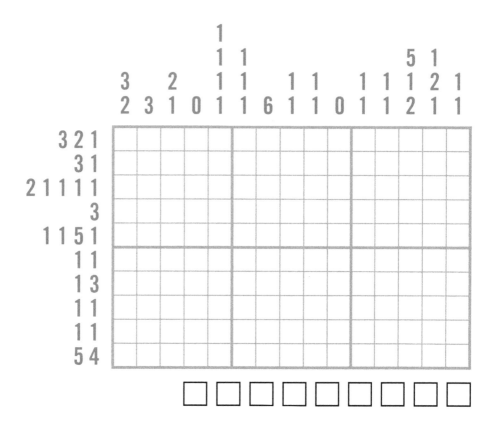

 Answer on page 168

HINT: A rebus is a representation of a phrase using pictures or symbols, so the code reference won't be needed for this puzzle.

	6		8	7	9	1		
8	9		2			4		
2						7		
9		8					5	
			6	3				
		3		8	7			
	1	5		6			8	7
	2		7	9				3
			3			6		4

See directions on page 6

HINT: 4th row, 5th column: NE

NONOGRAM 78

On the Trail

See directions on page 8

```
                    2   1 1             1   2
                    1   1 1       2       1 1 2 1
            1 1 9 1 2     1 1 7 1 2 1 1 1
            3 1 4 1 2 1 10 1 1 3 3 1 1 2 2
            1 2 1 1 3 1 1 3 1 3 1 1 1 2 1

      2 1
    2 1 1
    3 1 1
  1 4 2 1
  1 2 4 2
1 2 1 1 2
1 1 1 1 1 1
    5 1 2
  4 1 1 1
  2 1 4 1
  1 2 2 3
1 2 1 2 1
  3 2 1 2
  1 1 4 2
4 1 1 1 2
```

HINT: Row 13: (2)3(1)2(1)2(1)2(1) Picture Description: Hiker

See directions on page 10

1-	5+	12x	2÷		1-
			6÷		
3-		6÷	20x	2-	
11+				3÷	
4÷		2-		13+	3-
	1-				

HINT: 13+ cage: 2 65

CRYPTIC PUZZLE 80

See directions on page 14

Curses

&!

$##$#

$$##$

#!#$

#$!##

†##&$#

##!###

#!####

###$$

%!

$# #! & #% #& % #$ $%

HINT: Each symbol on the left represents a number between 1 and 5 given by each line of the solved Masyu.

LOGIC GRID  81

See directions on page 12

A New Class of Puzzle

Adam and his classmates have moved on to the next grade, certainly older and hopefully wiser. Accounting for their new tastes in music, as well as their updated grades and favorite subjects, can you figure out who's who among this group of friends?

CLUES:

› Bianca loves history.

› The fan of classic music also likes science. Their grade is almost the same as the jazz enthusiast's.

› Adam earned a C, but Cindy earned an A.

› Eric earned a worse grade than the person who prefers English.

› David is something of a metalhead, while Cindy prefers electronic music.

› Adam's favorite class is math.

› David loves his English classes. He earned a slightly different grade than the jazz music fan.

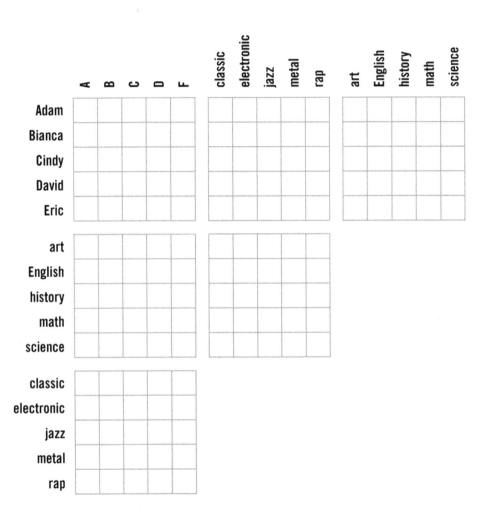

HINT: Eric earned a D.

MASYU 82

See directions on page 6

HINT: 6th row, 8th column: NE

NONOGRAM 83

Shredder

See directions on page 8

Column clues:

```
                                        1
        1                         2     1
        2                         2     1
        1                   1     1     1
        1  1     1    1     1  3     1     1
        1  4  1  3  1  1  3  5  1  4  2  1  3     1
        1  1  5  3  4  3  4  1  5  4  1  4  1  1  1
```

Row clues:

```
1 3 1 1 1 1 1
        1 1 1
      1 1 2 1
      1 1 5 2
      1 5 2 1
    1 2 1 1 1
      1 2 1 1
      1 1 2 1
    1 1 1 1 1
          1 1
    1 1 1 2 1
          1 1 5
    1 2 5 2 1
      1 2 1 1
  2 1 2 1 1 1
```

See directions on page 10

15+	1-		5-		5+
	12+		1-		
		2÷	30x	9+	11+
6x	4-				
		15x		10+	
	11+				

 Answer on page 168

HINT: 12+ cage: 5 4 3

CRYPTIC PUZZLE 85

See directions on page 14

To solve, see Code Sheet for Cryptic Puzzles on page 161.

Heads or Tails

8?		6?		45?
5x	9+			
		6x	80x	2+
7?	5?			
		3?		

□ □ □ □ □

Answer on page 169

HINT: "Heads or tails" is a binary choice, so you'll only need to choose between + and – for the unknown operations.

LOGIC GRID  86

See directions on page 12

The *Arr*-t of Puzzle Solving

Our band of fearsome pirates has uncovered another chest of booty to be distributed. Being an esoteric group of buccaneers, they've agreed to the following terms, based on their names, jacket colors, and current pirate-y possessions.

CLUES:

> Cursechin, who owns a parrot, receives more gold than the wearer of the brown jacket and almost as much gold as the owner of the cerulean jacket.

> Evilear doesn't have the treasure map.

> The least amount of gold goes to the wearer of the violet jacket.

> Blackbeard receives about as much gold as the owner of the hook for a hand, Arsonnose.

> The yellow-jacketed pirate receives more gold than Arsonnose.

> Arsonnose receives about the same amount of gold as the wielder of the cutlass. Darkeye receives about the same gold as the wearer of the violet jacket.

> *Awk!* Polly the parrot has 300 gold coins! *Awk!*

	100 gold	200 gold	300 gold	400 gold	500 gold	brown	cerulean	green	violet	yellow	cutlass	eyepatch	hook hand	parrot	treasure map
Arsonnose															
Blackbeard															
Cursechin															
Darkeye															
Evilear															
cutlass															
eyepatch															
hook hand															
parrot															
treasure map															
brown															
cerulean															
green															
violet															
yellow															

HINT: Darkeye receives 200 gold coins.

See directions on page 4

						5		3
		5					8	
7			1		3	6		
		4		7	8	1		2
	9	7						5
			6	4		7		
9	7			2			5	
6		3		8			4	
1				3			7	9

Marks the Spot

Column clues:
```
                2               1
                4     3         2     2
        6 2     1 3 2       2   1       1
    5 2 3 2 1 4 1 2 5 1 2 1 7 1
    4 2 2 10 1 4 1 2 4 2 6 2 2 4 4
    3 2 2 1 1 1 2 8 2 1 5 1 3 1 10
```

Row clues:
```
2 3 2 2 2
    11 1 1
3 2 2 2 1
2 2 3 3 1
2 3 2 1 2
  1 4 4 1
  1 9 1 1
4 1 2 3 1
    5 5 2
1 1 1 2 4
      7 6
3 1 1 2 2
1 6 1 1 1
3 3 1 1 1
      6 6
```

CALCUDOKU 89

See directions on page 10

1-	24x		2÷	24x	1-
		3-			
2-			2-		24x
2÷	20x				
	12+		12x		3÷
2-			11+		

Answer on page 169

HINT: 12+ cage: 65 1

CRYPTIC PUZZLE 90

See directions on page 14

To solve, see Code Sheet for Cryptic Puzzles on page 161.

Face the Flags

CLUES:

- The hour 8 is used after the minutes :50.
- The hour 1 is used after the hour 8.
- The minutes :15 are used adjacent to the hour 7.
- The minutes :01 are used before the minutes :50.
- The minutes :00 are used after the hour 1.
- The hour 7 is used adjacent to the hour 10.

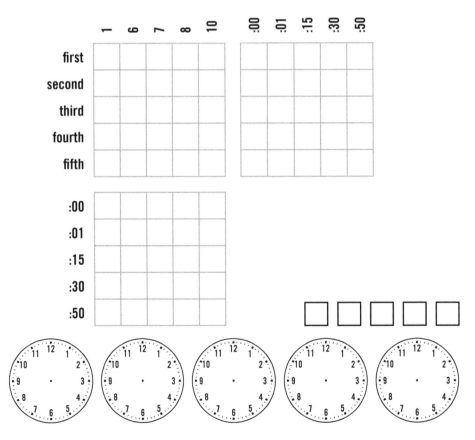

HINT: The logic grid solves to five times of day. Which code in the reference is most like a "face" clock?

LOGIC GRID  91

See directions on page 12

Where the Heart Is

This homeowner's association is out of control. Our friends Alice, Bob, Carl, Diana, and Eve didn't read the fine print, so they have been forced to rearrange houses and paint colors, all based upon their favorite beverages. Hopefully they at least have a nice community pool...

CLUES:

- The person who prefers milk lives to the right of the green house.
- The coffee drinker lives in a yellow house.
- Bob lives next to a non-ivory house, home to someone who loves milk.
- The middle house is painted green and doesn't contain even a drop of orange juice.
- The tea drinker lives next door to Bob.
- Carl lives in a blue house.
- Eve lives in the second house from the right.
- Diana lives near a yellow house.

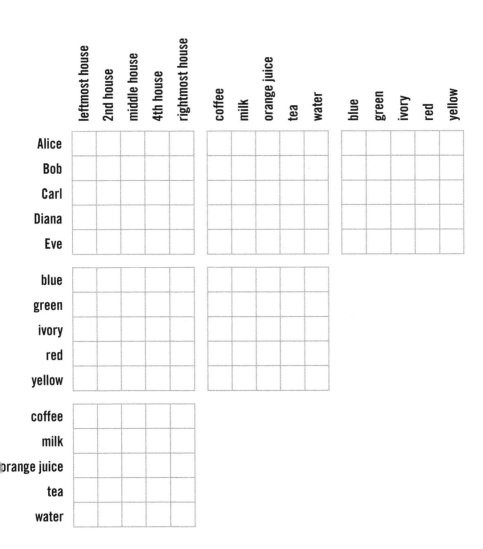

				8	7			
	8	9		2			5	
		6			3			7
1	4				9			
					6		2	1
	5	3				7		9
						6		
5			1	3				8
8		7				3		

HINT: Row 7: 231 798 645

See directions on page 6

HINT: 9th row, 3rd column: SE

CALCUDOKU 94

See directions on page 10

18+		24x		4-		2-
		3÷	5-	18+		
42x	30x					11+
		56x	5-	12+		
					72x	
3÷	360x		40x			5-

HINT: 18+ cage: 25 47

CRYPTIC PUZZLE 95

See directions on page 14

Evens Out, but Don't Double-Count

TIP

⊙ My remaining cryptic puzzles aren't related to the other puzzle types found in this book, but by using creativity and logic, you will still be able to extract their hidden solutions. Don't forget that each puzzle's title may be a hint on how to solve it.

V	T	E	A	R	K	S
E	M	E	I	V	L	E
I	R	I	Y	O	F	N
O	E	U	H	R	E	T
R	H	V	L	R	E	I
T	N	T	E	E	G	R

☐ ☐ ☐ ☐ ☐

HINT: A message appears by reading every other letter, starting with T.

LOGIC GRID  96

Dinner Is Served

Alvin and company never did get dinner at their last meetup due to someone else taking their reservation. Determined to not let this happen again, they've put their new reservation under both their first and last names. It's up to you to match those names together, along with their updated hobbies, shoe colors, and arrival order.

CLUES:

> Vanderbilt wears green shoes.

> Carol's shoes are not white.

> Yamaguchi arrived just before or after the person wearing purple shoes.

> Doug has recently joined a band. Vanderbilt arrived later than he did.

> Carol arrived at almost the same time as the photography hobbyist.

> Erin isn't wearing white shoes.

> Vanderbilt arrived before the purple shoe owner, but the crimson shoe owner arrived earlier still.

> The hiker arrived just before or after Alvin.

> Xavier arrived after Doug.

> The fourth person to arrive brought their camera, while the third person brought white shoes.

> The cook arrived at almost the same time as Bart.

> Erin arrived just before or after Yamaguchi.

> Zale arrived last.

> Alvin arrived at almost the same time as the person wearing crimson shoes.

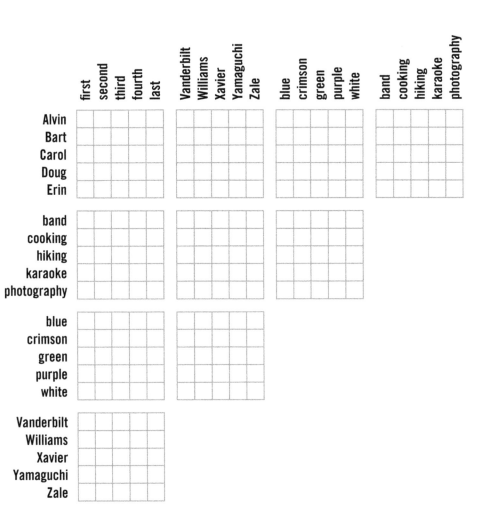

HINT: Bart arrived third.

SUDOKU 97

See directions on page 4

	6					2		4
7		8	4	1		3		
						8		
1		5					7	8
				3	5		4	
	4				9			1
	2		6				8	9
	5	4	9	8				
9					1			6

HINT: Column 2: 691 374 258

See directions on page 6

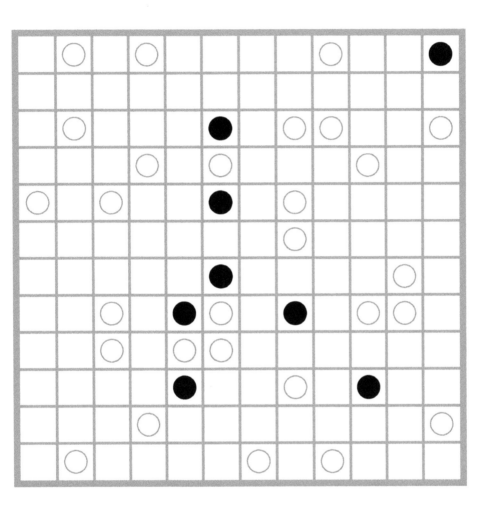

HINT: 8th row, 5th column: NE

NONOGRAM 99

King Me

See directions on page 8

Column clues (top):

```
                1           2
        1       1       1   1       1       1           1
        3   1   1       1   1   1       1       3       1   1               1   1
    1   1   1   1   1   1   3   1   1   1   1   1       1   1   3   3   1   1
    3   1   1   1   3   1   3   1   3   1   1   1   3   2   1   2   1   1   1
    3   1   3   1   3   1   3   1   3   1   3   1   1   2   4   2   1
    1   1   3   1   3   1   1   1   3   1   3   1   1   3   1   2   1   1   1
```

Row clues (left):

```
    1 2 4 1 1 2 2
      1 1 1 1 4 1
          2 1 2 2
          2 3 5 2
      3 1 1 1 2 1 1
        2 3 3 1 2
    1 1 1 1 1 1 1 1
        3 3 3 1 1 2
  1 1 1 1 1 1 1 1 1 1
        2 3 3 3 3
    1 1 1 1 1 1 1 3 1
        3 3 3 1 1 1
    1 1 1 1 1 1 1 1
          3 3 2 1
      2 1 1 1 1 2 2 1
```

HINT: Column 2: (1)(1)(3)(1)(1)(3)(1)(1)(2)1
Picture Description: Checkers

CALCUDOKU 100

See directions on page 10

13+	1-		10+		10+	2-
		12+				
5-		9+		3-	1-	
8+		2÷			13+	
3-	7÷		3÷		20x	
	12x		7+		1-	6-
140x			2÷			

HINT: Upper 13+ cage: 4, 27

117

CRYPTIC PUZZLE 101

See directions on page 14

Love Connection

Mark the names in the grid to reveal five large letters.

ASHTON   DYLAN   JAMIE   LESLIE   PEYTON

CASEY   HARLEY   KAI   NICKY   SAM

		A	C	G		F	X	S		
	Y	E	S	N	E	L	E	X	N	A	B
	♡	J	Y	H	S	O	Z	R	L	L	K
	J	A	M	S	L	I	E	♡	D	Y	K
E	F	H	I	E	B	U	N	S	Q	U	R	W
R	Z	T	O	N	♡	P	K	Y	E	R	H	A
K	V	H	Q	Z	B	E	A	N	L	R	J	S
	G	S	N	O	T	Y	I	I	T	A	N
		A	K	R	S	T	♡	C	♡	H
			L	G	Z	H	S	K	Y
				O	V	G	A	D
					J	G	M
						L

☐ ☐ ☐ ☐ ☐

HINT: Each name appears in the grid of letters, but not necessarily in a straight line.

See directions on page 4

			8		9			
1			5			7		
7		9					5	6
				3				
	6	5					1	4
				2		3	6	5
9						6		
6	4	2		9				
				6	2		7	8

LOGIC GRID 103

Third Time's the Charm

Aiden and friends have decided to run one last pentathlon, and this time the stakes are high. They've each enlisted the support of a corporate sponsor: VENN.biz, WILE LLC, XYLO Coop, YAMM Ltd., and ZORO Corp. They've also swapped up their athletic specialties and shirt colors, and it's up to you to determine in what order they finished.

CLUES:

- Chloe finished after the archery expert and racer sponsored by YAMM, but before the biking expert.

- The racer wearing black finished just before Everett.

- The best swimmer finished immediately before or after the racer wearing gray.

- The overall winner wore pink, while the racer in cyan finished in third.

- The racer sponsored by VENN placed just before or after the swimming expert.

- The fencing specialist finished after Aiden.

- The best biker finished just before or after Diego and sometime before the racer sponsored by VENN.

- XYLO is a well-known supporter of fencers.

- The racer sponsored by WILE finished after Diego.

- The best swimmer didn't wear pink or cyan.

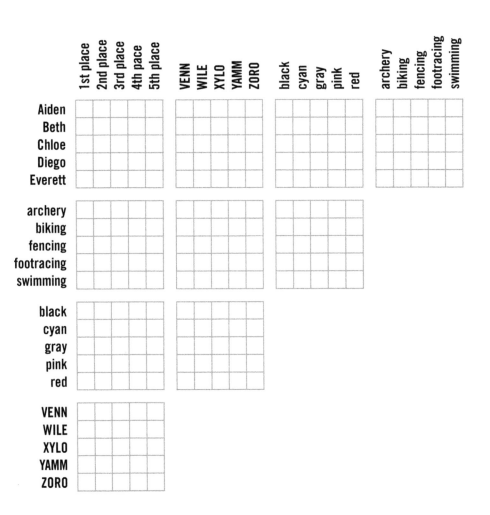

HINT: Chloe finished second.

See directions on page 6

HINT: 8th row, 9th column: NE

NONOGRAM 105

Sandy Graves

See directions on page 8

Column clues (top):

```
                    1                         2           2
        1 3       4 3     5 3 1           1 2       2 2
        6 7 4 7 4 3 3   1 2 2     4 2 4 2 1 4 4 1
        3 1 1 2 1 1 1 7 1 1 1 3 2 3 1 1 1 2 1 2
        2 1 1 1 1 2 1 2 1 1 2 4 2 1 1 2 1 2 1 1
```

Row clues (left):

```
    4 6 1 3 1
    1 4 3 2 4
       10 1 2
    2 6 1 1 1
    5 3 1 1 1
  4 1 1 1 2 1
  3 1 2 1 2 1
  3 1 1 1 1 1
    2 1 2 1 2
    1 1 2 5
       1 3 2
    4 7 1 1
2 1 2 1 1 1 1
1 2 2 1 2 1 1
1 2 2 1 1 1 2
```

HINT: Row 13: 1(1)1(1)2(1)2(1)1(1)2(1)1(2)

Picture Description: Pyramids

123

CALCUDOKU 106

See directions on page 10

3-		252x	30x		21x	
4-			5+		28x	
7+			11+	2÷	4÷	
4-					4-	
12x	24x			14+		
	70x			48x		2÷
4-		5÷				

HINT: 48x cage: 16 42

CRYPTIC PUZZLE 107

See directions on page 14

To solve, see Code Sheet for Cryptic Puzzles on page 161.

Crimson Crisscross

It's easy to see how to fill BLOOD, ROSE, and WINE into the puzzle below, even if you can't.

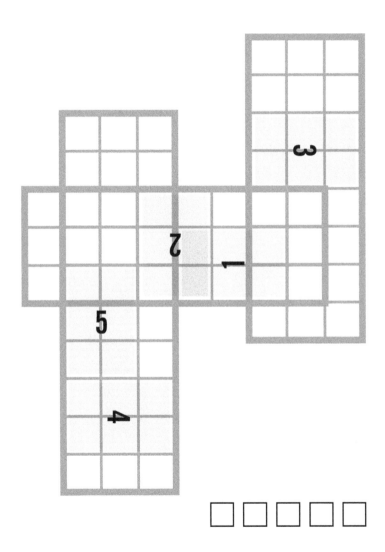

HINT: Each word should be written in Braille before filling into the puzzle.

LOGIC GRID  108

See directions on page 12

We'll Be Right Back After These Messages

In the cutthroat world of modern television production, studios really need to prepare for possible spin-off shows including young versions of their lead characters. To this end, our studio shopping around Alpha et al. has retooled each show to have a (possibly) new genre and public access station and assigned each show a spin-off program with a working title of Victor, Whiskey, X-ray, Yankee, or Zulu. Can you figure out their new ratings?

CLUES:

- The game show received the second-best ratings, but the news show did even better.
- The talk show is shown on WULV and received almost the same ratings as Alpha.
- The drama did about as well as WSBA's show in the ratings.
- Delta received slightly different ratings than the show whose spinoff is named Whiskey.
- Bravo did better than the game show in the ratings.
- X-ray spun off from a show on WTCC.
- Charlie isn't a news show, but it did almost as well in the ratings.
- Victor spun off from Echo, which ended up in the middle of the ratings.
- Bravo performed about as well as the show on WQKG.
- The game show received lower ratings than the show with the spin-off named Yankee.

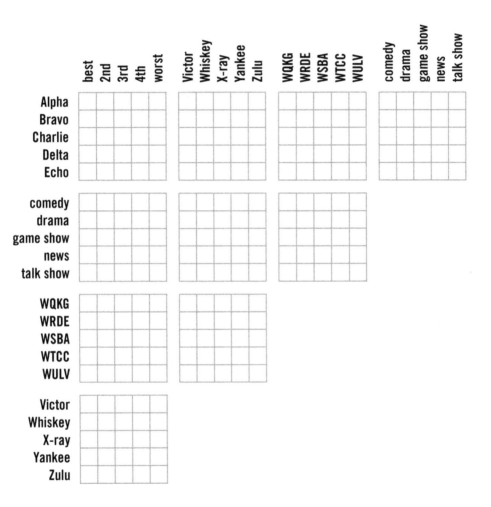

See directions on page 4

		5				7	8	
1	2							6
9					5		2	
		6		1				8
	1		8	7				
	7			4		3		2
3			7			2	6	4
	6	2	3					
	9	8	4					3

HINT: Column 4: 196 285 734

See directions on page 6

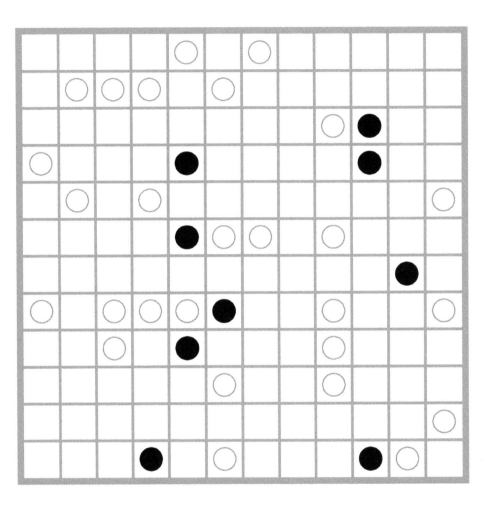

HINT: 4th row, 5th column: NE

Do You?

See directions on page 8

										1	1	1		2				1	
	4		3	2	1	1		1	1	1	1		1			3	1	
5	1	3	1	1	1	1	1	1	1	1	1	5	1	1	2	1	1	6
1	2	1	2	1	3	2	1	3	1	1	4	1	2	1	1	2	1	1
1	1	3	2	1	1	1	1	1	4	4	1	1	1	1	1	1	3	1	3
2	1	1	1	2	4	5	5	5	1	1	1	1	1	2	1	1	1	1

Row clues:

```
        7 3 3 2
        5 3 2 2 1
        4 2 4 1 1
      2 1 1 1 2 1
        1 2 5 5 2
    1 2 1 1 1 1 1
  1 1 2 1 1 1 1 1
  2 1 2 1 1 1 1 1
        3 2 2 1 1
        2 1 5 1 1 1
        1 6 1 1 1
    2 1 6 1 2 1 1
        1 1 5 1 1
        1 5 1 2 1 1
        1 5 1 1 1 2
```

HINT: Column 6: 1(1)1(2)3(1)1(1)4   Picture Description: Bride

CALCUDOKU 112

See directions on page 10

8+	12+		3-		1-	
	6÷		3÷		1-	
13+		2-		9+		
		2-	3-		2-	2÷
336x			5÷			
		10+	15x	9+		6÷
				2-		

HINT: 336x cage: 27 64

131

See directions on page 14

Compass Rose

- BERGENIA: SE-SE-SE-E-NW-NE-W
- DAISY: NE-SE-NE-NE
- MARIGOLD: S-SW-SW-N-W-W-NW
- POPPY: SW-SE-W-W
- VIOLET: W-SE-W-SW-SW

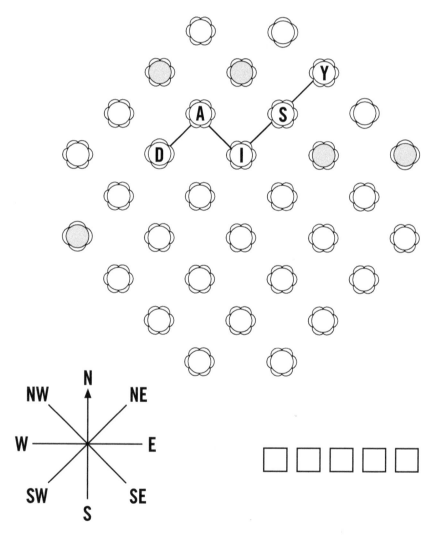

HINT: Each word begins on a flower with four petals. Each flower should contain a letter from exactly one of the words.

See directions on page 4

7	9							1
	6	5						7
				9	8	5		4
	2	4				7	8	9
	8		6	2		3		
5	1						2	
8		9		5		1		
		6			1		7	
2		1	8		9		5	

HINT: Column 8: 396 812 475

See directions on page 6

HINT: 8th row, 5th column: SE

NONOGRAM 116

All the Way Down

See directions on page 8

```
                              1           1
                    1  1  1      1  1  1      1  1  1  1  1  1  1  2
                 2  2  1  1  2  1  1  1  1  1  1  1  2  1  2  1  2  3  5
                 3  2  1  2  2  1  1  2  3  1  1  1  2  2  2  2  2  2  7
                 2  1  1  2  1  1  2  2  1  2  1  3  1  1  1  1  1  3  2  2
                 3  2  2  3  4  4  3  1  2  1  1  1  2  1  1  1  1  1  2

     2 1 2 1 2 5
     1 1 2 1 2 4
     1 1 1 1 1 3
     2 1 2 1 1 2
     2 1 1 1 1 2
     1 5 1 2 1 1
     1 1 1 1 1 1
     1 1 5 1 1 1
     2 1 1 1 1 1
     1 4 2 1 1 1
     1 4 1 1 3 1
     2 2 1 3 1 2
       1 4 1 2 1
     7 1 1 1 1 1
     8 2 1 3 2
```

HINT: Column 13: 1(1)1(1)2(2)2(2)1(1)1 Picture Description: Turtle

LOGIC GRID  117

The Office (UK)

While this puzzle may seem similar to earlier office-themed puzzles, there are some distinct differences. Sure, Alice and her colleagues are still involved, along with (reassigned) security levels A through E and five company departments. But in the UK, the bottom floor is called the ground floor, putting the first floor one story higher. If that's not enough variety, I've also factored in how long each employee has worked at the office, adding one more dimension of challenge from before.

CLUES:

- Having an office on the ground floor requires security clearance level D.
- Chris is on the second floor, just above or below marketing.
- The employee who has worked here for three months has C-level security clearance and works just above the ground floor.
- Supply chain management doesn't require A-level security.
- The person who has worked here for seven years is just above or below Beth, while the person who has worked here for two years is just above or below Anna.
- Dean works in marketing.
- Everyone in human resources has worked for the company for a decade, but the supply chain management worker has only been here four years.
- The floor requiring security clearance level D is just above or below accounting, but the floor requiring security clearance level E is just above or below Chris's office.
- The employee with two years' experience works on almost the same floor as supply chain management.
- Anna doesn't have B-level security clearance.

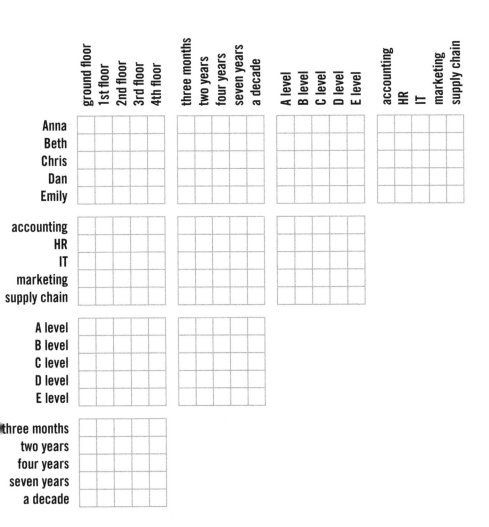

HINT: Emily works on the ground floor.

CALCUDOKU 118

See directions on page 10

2÷		14x		4÷		1-
56x	4-		30x	12+		
					12+	1-
12+	3÷	24x				
		2-		3-		13+
24x	9+	3÷		525x	7+	

HINT: 56x cage: 2 147

CRYPTIC PUZZLE 119

See directions on page 14

To solve, see Code Sheet for Cryptic Puzzles on page 161.

Electronic Mail

Subj: Use AEIOU for one

ALONE

BRAVE

AGREE

REACT

PHONE

SCUBA

SUEDE

ACORN

TABLE

ABORT

SWARM

BRIBE

GHOST

OTTER

LOOMS

INDIA

HINT: Emails are sent and received by computers as a series of Os and 1s.

139

See directions on page 4

9	8					4		
	2		7	8	9			
5			4					
1		2		6	4	8		
4		5						
				3	1	5		6
	7	9		4	2	6	3	
		1	6		3	9	8	
3		6		7			2	

HINT: Row 7: 879 142 635

HINT: 10th row, 7th column: NE

141

Have You Seen Ms. Sandiego?

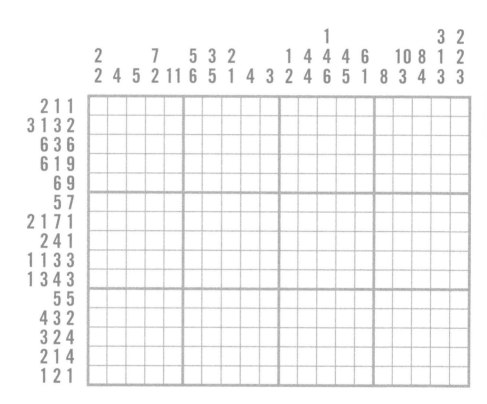

HINT: Row 9: 1(3)1(6)3(1)3(2)   Picture Description: Atlas

CALCUDOKU 123

See directions on page 10

10+		35x	2-	10+		2-
5÷	30x			5-		
		2-	4-		28x	
3÷			28x		10+	4-
	5-	10+	9+			
3-				4-	21x	
	40x				2÷	

HINT: 30x cage: 2 5 3

LOGIC GRID  124

See directions on page 12

Making the Grade

It's senior year, and classmates Adam, Bianca, Cindy, David, and Eric are now looking forward to graduation. They plan to celebrate with their best friends Violet, Will, Xander, Yvonne, and Zelda. Based on their current grades, favorite subjects, and musical preferences, I'll let you determine who will be hanging out with whom when the mortarboards are tossed in the air (and who will be spending the summer repeating their last required course).

CLUES:

- Bianca's grade is almost the same as Zelda's best friend's.
- The metalhead's grade is one letter better or worse than the student who enjoys math most.
- You won't find any classical music on a smartphone owned by the student taking extra history classes.
- The student who prefers art earned a B; Zelda's best friend's grade was only slightly different.
- Eric's grade is one letter better or worse than the fan of history class.
- Adam's best friend is Yvonne.
- Violet's best friend isn't taking art classes.
- The fan of rap music got an A, while David did almost as well but not quite.
- Will's best friend got a better grade than the fan of classical music.
- The locker of the student who likes science best is filled with posters of jazz musicians; its owner earned almost the same grade as the fan of classical music.

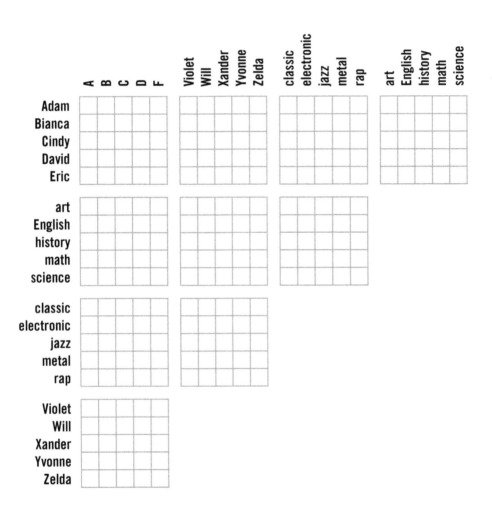

HINT: Bianca earned a D. **145**

CRYPTIC PUZZLE 125

See directions on page 14

The Queens' Many Names

a5: IETN IGHTFIVE IHNOF INNE ITVEE
b3: EE EEN EHGNYI ENTHIRT ENY ERTREE ET EV
c1: TEV TNE TNNRHTNN TOHEVE TYFIVE
d7: IE IHTETOY IN INETE INYT IRILT IT ITGT
e2: NETW NF NHEFRNT NI NILE NONEE NTRGE NY
f8: WEEIEIEI WEN WNHHHV WTE WTENIN
g6: EE EE EE EERHTNE EET EIETNN ETE EVLRTV
h4: EEEEN ELEEERHT EREF ETWE EVENE

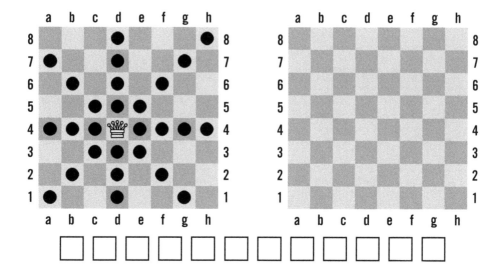

See directions on page 4

8	9			5				
2			7		9			
		4			3			
		9	6		2			3
					1	8	9	7
	1	5	9	7				
	5		2			7		
			3			4		1
	4	2		9		5		

See directions on page 6

HINT: 3rd row, 9th column: SE

NONOGRAM 128

See directions on page 8

Not-So-Small Wonder

Column clues:
```
                1 1 1                   1
        4       1 1 1                   3           2
        2         1 1 1 1 1             2           2
  1 3 1 4 2 1 1 1 1 1 1 1 1 1 2 4 1 3       1
  7 2 1 1 1 4 1 2 1 1 1 2 1 4 1 1 1 2 8 2
  1 6 1 7 2 7 2 2 1 1 1 2 2 7 1 7 1 6 1 4
```

Row clues:
```
    2 4 1 6 1
    4 2 2 2 3
      4 2 2 4
  1 2 1 1 2 2
      3 2 2 4
  2 1 1 1 1 2
    1 1 7 1 2
  1 1 1 1 1 1
    1 3 3 3 2
    5 1 1 1 3 1
2 1 1 5 1 1 2
    3 1 1 3 1
1 1 3 1 1 1 1
3 1 1 1 1 3 1
1 1 5 1 1 1 1
```

I Hope You *Arr*-n't Tired of Pirate Puns

The fearsome pirate Arsonnose and his fellow buccaneers have plundered a final cache of treasure, obviously to be distributed based upon the following arbitrary requirements. In addition to their names, pirate-y possessions, and coat colors, their home ports have been added as a final variable to consider.

CLUES:

- The pirate hailing from Orange Bay receives about as much gold as the pirate wearing violet.

- Blackbeard receives more gold than the parrot's owner.

- The pirate wearing yellow receives about as much as the pirate using a hook for a hand.

- The pirate hailing from St. Mary's receives 300 gold coins, while Cursechin receives 500 pieces.

- The pirate wielding a cutlass receives 100 more or less pieces of gold than Arsonnose, who wears an eyepatch.

- Darkeye receives about the same amount of gold as the owner of the parrot.

- New Providence's least favorite son receives a slightly different amount of gold than Blackbeard does.

- The pirate from Orange Bay receives less gold than the pirate wearing green.

- Evilear receives about as much treasure as the pirate wearing an eyepatch.

- The owner of the treasure map deserves more gold than the pirate wearing brown, who in turn will receive more than the pirate from Tortuga.

- The pirate from New Providence receives about as much gold as the pirate wearing green.

- The parrot's owner receives 200 gold coins, while the pirate wearing green receives 400.

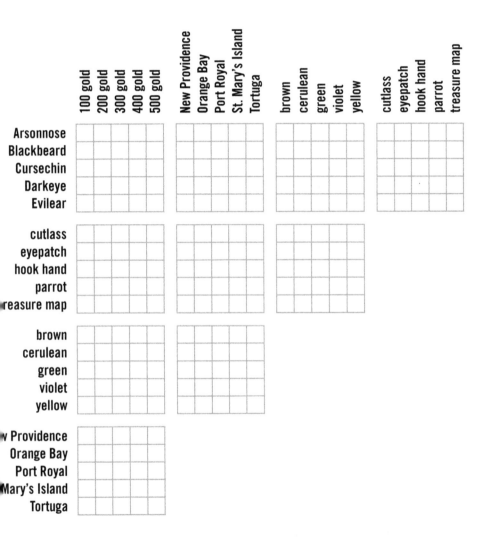

	100 gold	200 gold	300 gold	400 gold	500 gold	New Providence	Orange Bay	Port Royal	St. Mary's Island	Tortuga	brown	cerulean	green	violet	yellow	cutlass	eyepatch	hook hand	parrot	treasure map
Arsonnose																				
Blackbeard																				
Cursechin																				
Darkeye																				
Evilear																				
cutlass																				
eyepatch																				
hook hand																				
parrot																				
treasure map																				
brown																				
cerulean																				
green																				
violet																				
yellow																				
New Providence																				
Orange Bay																				
Port Royal																				
St. Mary's Island																				
Tortuga																				

CALCUDOKU 130

See directions on page 10

48x	10x		13+		21x	4÷
	15x		1-			
		6-		13+		
20x			1-		2-	12+
36x			28x			
21+		12+		4-		1-
				4-		

HINT: 28x cage: 71 4

CRYPTIC PUZZLE 131

See directions on page 14

The Puzzler's Apprentice

Help the puzzlemaster's assistant find her way to the center of her master's maze, formed by the following rules.

CLUES:

- Traveling on a square marked with a number is forbidden.
- Each number gives the size of the connected group of forbidden squares that includes it.
- Likewise, each connected group of forbidden squares contains exactly one number and cannot touch another group except diagonally.
- Every 2-by-2 group of squares includes at least one forbidden square.
- The non-forbidden squares form a single connected group.

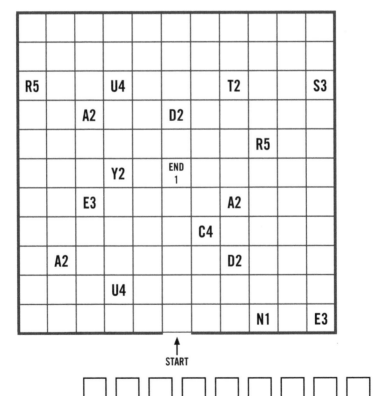

HINT: As the apprentice travels the maze, she will be able to spell out the solution to the puzzle.

			7		9		5	
		8		3			4	1
6		3						
					2		9	
8			6	4				
		1						
	1			9				
7	8					5		3
	2		1		3			7

HINT: Column 2: 475 693 182

See directions on page 6

HINT: 7th row, 7th column: SE

155

NONOGRAM 134

Smarty-Pants

See directions on page 8

Column clues:

```
                    1
              1 1 3                 1
              3 3 1       1 1   2       1 1   1
              1 1 1 1     1 2   1       1 3 1 3
          1 1 2 1 1 7   2 1 4 1       1 1 3 1 1
          1 1 1 1 1 1   1 3 2 2 1     1 1 1 1 1
        7 5 1 1 1 1 1   1 1 1 1 1 3 7 2 3 2 1 1
        3 1 3 3 3 1 1 1 3 4 1 1 6 1 1 2 2 5 1 4
        7 1 1 1 1 1 7 3 5 1 2 1 5 2 1 1 2 2 2 1
```

Row clues:

```
       7 1 1 7
     1 1 1 1 1 1
 1 3 1 1 1 1 3 1
 1 3 1 2 1 1 3 1
   1 3 1 3 1 3 1
     1 1 3 1 1 1
       7 1 1 1 7
             3
     5 4 2 1 1 2
 2 1 1 2 2 2 1
     2 1 6 1 1
         3 1 5
     1 5 1 1 2 1
           6 6
     7 1 1 1 1 1
     1 1 1 2 2 1
     1 3 1 3 5 1
     1 3 1 2 2 2
     1 3 1 2 1 2
       1 1 1 1 3
       7 4 2 1
```

HINT: Row 4: 1(1)3(1)1(1)2(1)1(2)1(2)1(1)3(1)1

CALCUDOKU 135

See directions on page 10

7-		3-		11+		10+	3÷
2-	210x			5-			
		5+	80x			3-	
10x	16+		28x			11+	
		140x		1-		60x	8÷
		13+					
18+				8+	2-	10x	
		3-				3-	

HINT: 18+ cage: 78 12

LOGIC GRID 136

See directions on page 12

A Zebra Puzzle

My final logic grid puzzle brings to a close the odyssey of Alice and her neighbors, their homes, their home colors, their favorite drinks, and now their pets and favorite lollipop flavors.

CLUES:

- The dog owner, who lives to the right of the water drinker, doesn't like tea.
- The leftmost house is home to a fox.
- The homeowner who prefers raspberry lollipops lives to the right of the green house.
- The rightmost house, home to a tea drinker, is yellow and is next-door to the green house.
- A stash of cherry lollipops may be found in a house next-door to the yellow home.
- The person who enjoys milk the best also prefers peach lollipops.
- The zebra's owner lives in an ivory house next-door to a coffee afficionado.
- The horse's stable is attached to the middle house; Eve doesn't live there, though.
- The person who prefers water doesn't live in an ivory house.
- Bob doesn't drink coffee often, but his neighbor does.
- Alice likes raspberry candy, while the fox owner isn't a fan of tangerine flavor.
- The water drinker lives to the right of Diana; Bob lives to the right of the red house.

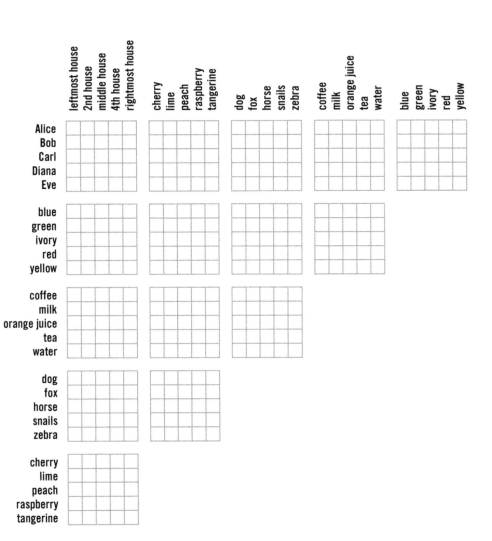

CRYPTIC PUZZLE 137

See directions on page 14

Complete the Square

TIP

▸ This is an example of a *metapuzzle*, which requires the solutions to all twenty-four previous Cryptic Puzzles. Good luck!

O	?
N	I

A	S
?	I

?	A
A	W

U	?
A	G

C	P
?	M

B	B
?	M

HINT: There's a unique way to fill in the answers from the 24 other Cryptic Puzzles into the crisscross. If done correctly, you can find the letters from each square as the corners of a larger square in the crisscross.

CODE SHEET FOR CRYPTIC PUZZLES

LETTER	DECIMAL (BASE 10)	BINARY (BASE 2)	MORSE	BRAILLE	SEMAPHORE	PIGPEN
A	1	00001				
B	2	00010				
C	3	00011				
D	4	00100				
E	5	00101				
F	6	00110				
G	7	00111				
H	8	01000				
I	9	01001				
J	10	01010				
K	11	01011				
L	12	01100				
M	13	01101				
N	14	01110				
O	15	01111				
P	16	10000				
Q	17	10001				
R	18	10010				
S	19	10011				
T	20	10100				
U	21	10101				
V	22	10110				
W	23	10111				
X	24	11000				
Y	25	11001				
Z	26	11010				

ANSWERS

PAGE 4 SUDOKU WARM-UP 1

9	7	8	6	2	4	1	5	3
5	3	1	9	8	7	2	6	4
6	4	2	5	1	3	8	9	7
7	8	9	4	6	5	3	1	2
1	2	3	7	9	8	6	4	5
4	5	6	1	3	2	9	7	8
3	6	5	2	4	1	7	8	9
2	1	4	8	7	9	5	3	6
8	9	7	3	5	6	4	2	1

PAGE 6 MASYU WARM-UP 2

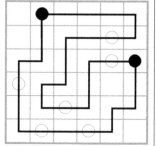

PAGE 8 NONOGRAM WARM-UP 3

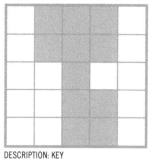

DESCRIPTION: KEY

PAGE 10 CALCUDOKU WARM-UP 4

2	1	3	4
1	4	2	3
3	2	4	1
4	3	1	2

PAGE 12 LOGIC GRID WARM-UP 5

First house: Carl, blue

Second house: Bob, green

Middle house: Diana, yellow

Fourth house: Alice, ivory

PAGE 14 CRYPTIC PUZZLE WARM-UP 6

Each letter in the sudoku puzzle solves to a different number between 1 and 9. These numbers spell out the solution BEGINNING.

PAGE 16 SUDOKU 7

1	3	2	6	5	4	7	8	9
7	9	8	3	2	1	4	5	6
4	6	5	9	8	7	1	2	3
3	5	6	7	9	8	2	1	4
8	7	9	4	1	2	3	6	5
2	4	1	5	6	3	8	9	7
5	1	3	2	4	6	9	7	8
6	2	4	8	7	9	5	3	1
9	8	7	1	3	5	6	4	2

PAGE 17 MASYU 8

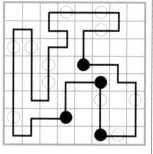

PAGE 18 NONOGRAM 9

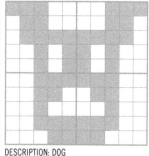

DESCRIPTION: DOG

PAGE 19 CALCUDOKU 10

5	2	4	1	3
3	5	2	4	1
2	4	1	3	5
4	1	3	5	2
1	3	5	2	4

PAGE 20 LOGIC GRID 11

First: Doug, band

Second: Carol, cooking

Third: Erin, karaoke

Fourth: Alvin, photography

Last: Bart, hiking

PAGE 21 CRYPTIC PUZZLE 12

Above each column, write the letter given by the row where 1 can be found. This spells the solution COUNT.

ANSWERS

PAGE 22 SUDOKU 13

5	4	6	8	9	7	1	3	2
2	1	3	5	6	4	7	9	8
8	7	9	2	3	1	4	6	5
6	3	5	9	7	8	2	4	1
9	8	7	1	4	2	3	5	6
1	2	4	6	5	3	8	7	9
4	6	2	7	8	9	5	1	3
7	9	8	3	1	5	6	2	4
3	5	1	4	2	6	9	8	7

PAGE 23 MASYU 14

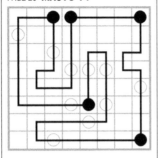

PAGE 24 NONOGRAM 15

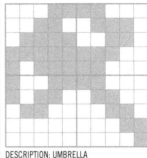

DESCRIPTION: UMBRELLA

PAGE 25 CALCUDOKU 16

4	1	3	5	2
1	3	5	2	4
3	5	2	4	1
2	4	1	3	5
5	2	4	1	3

PAGE 26 CRYPTIC PUZZLE 17

The solved Masyu path spells AVENUE.

PAGE 27 LOGIC GRID 18

First place: Beth, fencing
Second place: Aiden, footracing
Third place: Chloe, biking
Fourth place: Everett, archery
Last place: Diego, swimming

PAGE 28 SUDOKU 19

3	6	5	2	4	1	9	7	8
8	9	7	3	5	6	1	4	2
2	1	4	8	7	9	6	5	3
1	2	3	7	9	8	5	6	4
4	5	6	1	3	2	8	9	7
7	8	9	4	6	5	2	3	1
9	7	8	6	2	4	3	1	5
6	4	2	5	1	3	7	8	9
5	3	1	9	8	7	4	2	6

PAGE 29 MASYU 20

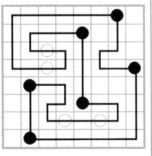

PAGE 30 NONOGRAM 21

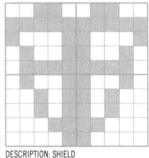

DESCRIPTION: SHIELD

PAGE 31 CALCUDOKU 22

2	5	3	1	4
5	3	1	4	2
4	2	5	3	1
1	4	2	5	3
3	1	4	2	5

PAGE 32 LOGIC GRID 23

Best ratings: Delta, comedy
Second-best ratings: Alpha, talk show
Middle-rated: Echo, drama
Second-worst ratings: Charlie, game show
Worst ratings: Bravo, news

PAGE 33 CRYPTIC PUZZLE 24

The first letters of each name spell the solution ACRONYM when ordered left to right, according to the logic grid puzzle.

ANSWERS

PAGE 34 SUDOKU 25

3	1	5	8	9	7	2	4	6
4	2	6	1	5	3	8	7	9
7	8	9	2	6	4	1	3	5
2	3	1	9	7	8	6	5	4
8	9	7	6	4	5	3	2	1
5	6	4	3	1	2	9	8	7
6	5	3	4	2	1	7	9	8
9	7	8	5	3	6	4	1	2
1	4	2	7	8	9	5	6	3

PAGE 35 MASYU 26

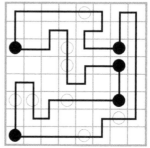

PAGE 36 NONOGRAM 27

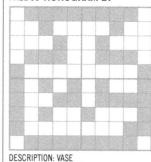

DESCRIPTION: VASE

PAGE 37 CALCUDOKU 28

5	1	3	2	4
1	2	4	3	5
4	5	2	1	3
3	4	1	5	2
2	3	5	4	1

PAGE 38 CRYPTIC PUZZLE 29

Using the capital from the nonogram solution and the lowercase not filled in in the grid, the solution PICTURE is spelled out.

PAGE 39 SUDOKU 30

5	6	4	2	3	1	8	7	9
2	3	1	8	9	7	5	4	6
8	9	7	5	6	4	2	1	3
3	1	5	7	8	9	4	6	2
7	8	9	4	2	6	3	5	1
4	2	6	3	1	5	7	9	8
9	7	8	6	5	3	1	2	4
1	4	2	9	7	8	6	3	5
6	5	3	1	4	2	9	8	7

PAGE 40 MASYU 31

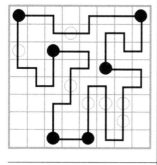

PAGE 41 NONOGRAM 32

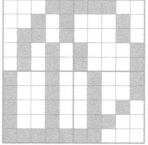

DESCRIPTION: TENT

PAGE 42 CALCUDOKU 33

1	3	4	5	2
3	5	1	2	4
5	2	3	4	1
4	1	2	3	5
2	4	5	1	3

PAGE 43 LOGIC GRID 34

First floor: Chris, human resources

Second floor: Emily, accounting

Third floor: Beth, information technology

Fourth floor: Anna, supply chain management

Fifth floor: Dean, marketing

PAGE 44 CRYPTIC PUZZLE 35

The diagonal of the solved sudoku puzzle spells UNEASIEST.

PAGE 45 SUDOKU 36

9	8	7	2	3	1	5	6	4
3	2	1	5	6	4	8	9	7
6	5	4	8	9	7	2	3	1
7	9	8	1	4	2	6	5	3
5	6	3	9	7	8	1	4	2
4	1	2	6	5	3	9	7	8
1	3	5	4	2	6	7	8	9
8	7	9	3	1	5	4	2	6
2	4	6	7	8	9	3	1	5

ANSWERS

PAGE 46 MASYU 37

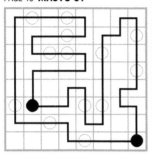

PAGE 47 NONOGRAM 38

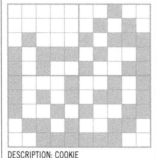

DESCRIPTION: COOKIE

PAGE 48 CRYPTIC PUZZLE 39

Reading top to bottom, left to right, the squares not used in the Masyu solution spell IMMACULATE.

PAGE 49 LOGIC GRID 40

A: Eric, history

B: Adam, science

C: Bianca, English

D: David, mathematics

F: Cindy, art

PAGE 50 MASYU 41

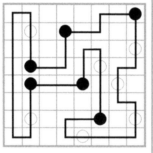

PAGE 51 NONOGRAM 42

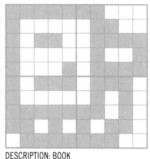

DESCRIPTION: BOOK

PAGE 52 CALCUDOKU 43

3	4	5	1	2
1	2	3	4	5
5	1	2	3	4
4	5	1	2	3
2	3	4	5	1

PAGE 53 LOGIC GRID 44

100 gold: Cursechin, hook hand

200 gold: Blackbeard, parrot

300 gold: Arsonnose, eyepatch

400 gold: Evilear, cutlass

500 gold: Darkeye, treasure map

PAGE 54 CRYPTIC PUZZLE 45

Ordering by the numbers 1 through 5, the lowercase letters given by valid relationships spell GREEK.

PAGE 55 SUDOKU 46

7	9	8	2	3	1	5	4	6
4	6	5	8	9	7	2	1	3
1	3	2	5	6	4	8	7	9
8	7	9	1	4	2	6	3	5
3	5	6	9	7	8	1	2	4
2	4	1	6	5	3	9	8	7
6	2	4	7	8	9	3	5	1
5	1	3	4	2	6	7	9	8
9	8	7	3	1	5	4	6	2

PAGE 56 NONOGRAM 47

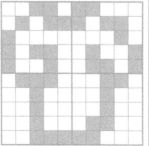

DESCRIPTION: SHIRT

PAGE 57 CALCUDOKU 48

1	5	3	4	2
3	2	5	1	4
4	3	1	2	5
2	1	4	5	3
5	4	2	3	1

ANSWERS

PAGE 58 CRYPTIC PUZZLE 49

The solution to the maze generated by the nonogram spells out the letters LABYRINTH.

PAGE 59 LOGIC GRID 50

First house: Alice, red

Second house: Diana, yellow

Middle house: Eve, blue

Fourth house: Bob, green

Last house: Carl, ivory

PAGE 60 SUDOKU 51

5	1	3	2	4	6	8	7	9
9	8	7	1	3	5	2	4	6
6	2	4	8	7	9	1	3	5
7	9	8	3	2	1	6	5	4
4	6	5	9	8	7	3	2	1
1	3	2	6	5	4	9	8	7
2	4	1	5	6	3	7	9	8
8	7	9	4	1	2	5	6	3
3	5	6	7	9	8	4	1	2

PAGE 61 MASYU 52

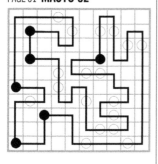

PAGE 62 CALCUDOKU 53

2	6	4	5	3	1
5	3	1	2	6	4
4	2	6	1	5	3
1	5	3	4	2	6
6	4	2	3	1	5
3	1	5	6	4	2

PAGE 63 CRYPTIC PUZZLE 54

The shaded cells in the solved Kenken, top to bottom, yield 7, 18, 1, 14, and 4, decoding to the word GRAND.

PAGE 64 LOGIC GRID 55

First: Erin, photography, green

Second: Alvin, cooking, blue

Third: Bart, band, purple

Fourth: Doug, karaoke, white

Last: Carol, hiking, crimson

PAGE 66 SUDOKU 56

1	5	3	2	4	6	7	8	9
8	9	7	1	3	5	4	2	6
2	6	4	8	7	9	3	1	5
3	1	2	6	5	4	8	9	7
6	4	5	9	8	7	2	3	1
9	7	8	3	2	1	5	6	4
7	8	9	4	1	2	6	5	3
5	3	6	7	9	8	1	4	2
4	2	1	5	6	3	9	7	8

PAGE 67 MASYU 57

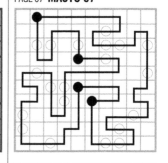

PAGE 68 NONOGRAM 58

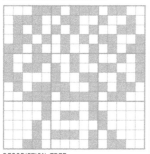

DESCRIPTION: TREE

PAGE 69 CRYPTIC PUZZLE 59

For each shaded region in the solved sudoku, replace the odd numbers with dashes and even numbers with dots. Top to bottom, this spells DASHED in Morse code.

PAGE 70 LOGIC GRID 60

First place: Beth, archery, black

Second place: Everett, biking, gray

Third place: Diego, fencing, cyan

Fourth place: Chloe, footracing, red

Last place: Aiden, swimming, pink

ANSWERS

PAGE 72 **MASYU 61**

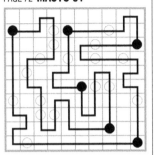

PAGE 73 **NONOGRAM 62**

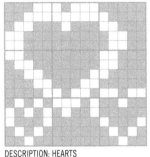

DESCRIPTION: HEARTS

PAGE 74 **CALCUDOKU 63**

2	1	5	6	4	3
1	6	4	5	3	2
3	2	6	1	5	4
6	5	3	4	2	1
5	4	2	3	1	6
4	3	1	2	6	5

PAGE 75 **CRYPTIC PUZZLE 64**

The left column of symbols matches the "pig" pen code; by filling in dots whenever the shaded cell is a valid relationship, the word PIGLET may be spelled.

PAGE 76 **LOGIC GRID 65**

Best ratings: Echo, drama, WTCC

Second-best ratings: Bravo, news, WQKG

Middle-rated: Delta, talk show, WULV

Second-worst ratings: Charlie, comedy, WRDE

Worst ratings: Alpha, game show, WSBA

PAGE 78 **SUDOKU 66**

3	5	6	4	1	2	8	9	7
2	4	1	7	9	8	3	6	5
8	7	9	5	6	3	2	1	4
4	6	5	3	2	1	7	8	9
1	3	2	9	8	7	4	5	6
7	9	8	6	5	4	1	2	3
5	1	3	8	7	9	6	4	2
6	2	4	1	3	5	9	7	8
9	8	7	2	4	6	5	3	1

PAGE 79 **MASYU 67**

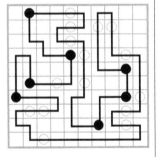

PAGE 80 **NONOGRAM 68**

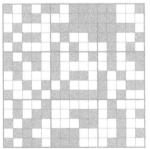

DESCRIPTION: SNOWMAN

PAGE 81 **CALCUDOKU 69**

1	6	3	5	4	2
6	5	2	4	3	1
5	4	1	3	2	6
4	3	6	2	1	5
3	2	5	1	6	4
2	1	4	6	5	3

PAGE 82 **CRYPTIC PUZZLE 70**

Using the cells passed through by each Masyu solution for each 3-by-2 rectangle, the word HAPPY is spelled in Braille.

PAGE 83 **SUDOKU 71**

1	4	2	6	5	3	7	8	9
9	7	8	1	4	2	5	3	6
6	5	3	9	7	8	4	2	1
7	8	9	3	1	5	2	6	4
3	1	5	4	2	6	8	9	7
4	2	6	7	8	9	1	5	3
5	6	4	8	9	7	3	1	2
8	9	7	2	3	1	6	4	5
2	3	1	5	6	4	9	7	8

PAGE 84 **MASYU 72**

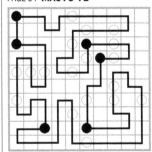

ANSWERS

PAGE 85 CALCUDOKU 73

3	6	1	5	4	2
2	5	6	4	3	1
6	3	4	2	1	5
5	2	3	1	6	4
1	4	5	3	2	6
4	1	2	6	5	3

PAGE 86 LOGIC GRID 74

First floor: Anna, human resources, C-level security

Second floor: Emily, accounting, A-level security

Third floor: Chris, information technology, D-level security

Fourth floor: Beth, supply chain management, E-level security

Fifth floor: Dean, marketing, B-level security

PAGE 88 CRYPTIC PUZZLE 75

The solved nonogram depicts the letter I followed by its shadow: that is, EYE SHADOW.

PAGE 89 SUDOKU 76

5	6	4	8	7	9	1	3	2
8	9	7	2	1	3	4	6	5
2	3	1	5	4	6	7	9	8
9	7	8	1	2	4	3	5	6
1	4	2	6	3	5	8	7	9
6	5	3	9	8	7	2	4	1
3	1	5	4	6	2	9	8	7
4	2	6	7	9	8	5	1	3
7	8	9	3	5	1	6	2	4

PAGE 90 MASYU 77

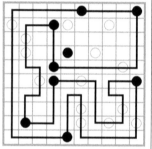

PAGE 91 NONOGRAM 78

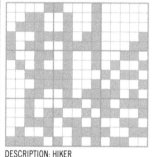

DESCRIPTION: HIKER

PAGE 92 CALCUDOKU 79

6	3	4	2	1	5
5	2	3	1	6	4
3	6	1	5	4	2
2	5	6	4	3	1
1	4	5	3	2	6
4	1	2	6	5	3

PAGE 93 CRYPTIC PUZZLE 80

Using the number of connected squares in each row of the solved Masyu puzzle, the symbols on the bottom of the puzzle decode to the numbers 21 14 3 15 13 5 12 25, spelling UNCOMELY.

PAGE 94 LOGIC GRID 81

A: Cindy, art, electronic

B: David, English, metal

C: Adam, mathematics, jazz

D: Eric, science, classic

F: Bianca, history, rap

PAGE 96 MASYU 82

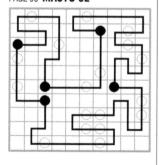

PAGE 97 NONOGRAM 83

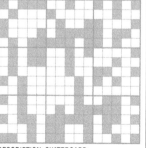

DESCRIPTION: SKATEBOARD

PAGE 98 CALCUDOKU 84

5	4	3	1	6	2
6	5	4	2	1	3
4	3	2	6	5	1
3	2	1	5	4	6
1	6	5	3	2	4
2	1	6	4	3	5

ANSWERS

PAGE 99 CRYPTIC PUZZLE 85

Using the operations × and + used in each row's cells and setting ×→0 and +→1, the resulting binary strings spell FLIPS.

PAGE 100 LOGIC GRID 86

100 gold: Evilear, eyepatch, violet

200 gold: Darkeye, treasure map, brown

300 gold: Cursechin, parrot, green

400 gold: Arsonnose, hook hand, cerulean

500 gold: Blackbeard, cutlass, yellow

PAGE 102 SUDOKU 87

4	2	6	8	9	7	5	1	3
3	1	5	2	6	4	9	8	7
7	8	9	1	5	3	6	2	4
5	6	4	9	7	8	1	3	2
8	9	7	3	1	2	4	6	5
2	3	1	6	4	5	7	9	8
9	7	8	4	2	1	3	5	6
6	5	3	7	8	9	2	4	1
1	4	2	5	3	6	8	7	9

PAGE 103 NONOGRAM 88

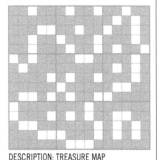

DESCRIPTION: TREASURE MAP

PAGE 104 CALCUDOKU 89

5	3	2	1	6	4
6	4	3	2	1	5
3	1	6	5	4	2
1	5	4	3	2	6
2	6	5	4	3	1
4	2	1	6	5	3

PAGE 105 CRYPTIC PUZZLE 90

Drawing the times 10:01, 7:50, 8:15, 1:30, and 6:00 as they appear on a face clock, the hands may be read using semaphore code as the word TIMED.

PAGE 106 LOGIC GRID 91

First house: Alice, yellow, coffee

Second house: Diana, ivory, tea

Middle house: Bob, green, water

Fourth house: Eve, red, milk

Last house: Carl, blue, orange juice

PAGE 108 SUDOKU 92

3	1	5	9	8	7	2	6	4
7	8	9	6	2	4	1	5	3
4	2	6	5	1	3	8	9	7
1	4	2	8	7	9	5	3	6
9	7	8	3	5	6	4	2	1
6	5	3	2	4	1	7	8	9
2	3	1	7	9	8	6	4	5
5	6	4	1	3	2	9	7	8
8	9	7	4	6	5	3	1	2

PAGE 109 MASYU 93

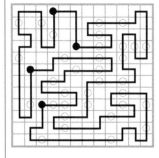

PAGE 110 CALCUDOKU 94

2	5	6	4	3	7	1
4	7	1	6	5	2	3
6	2	3	1	7	4	5
7	3	4	2	1	5	6
5	1	2	7	6	3	4
3	6	7	5	4	1	2
1	4	5	3	2	6	7

PAGE 111 CRYPTIC PUZZLE 95

The even-indexed letters read TAKE EVERY FOURTH LETTER. Not counting those letters again, every fourth letter gives the solution SIEVE.

PAGE 112 LOGIC GRID 96

First: Doug, band, crimson, Williams

Second: Alvin, cooking, green, Vanderbilt

Third: Bart, hiking, white, Yamaguchi

Fourth: Erin, photography, purple, Xavier

Last: Carol, karaoke, blue, Zale

ANSWERS

PAGE 114 **SUDOKU 97**

5	6	3	7	9	8	2	1	4
7	9	8	4	1	2	3	6	5
4	1	2	5	6	3	8	9	7
1	3	5	2	4	6	9	7	8
8	7	9	1	3	5	6	4	2
2	4	6	8	7	9	5	3	1
3	2	1	6	5	4	7	8	9
6	5	4	9	8	7	1	2	3
9	8	7	3	2	1	4	5	6

PAGE 115 **MASYU 98**

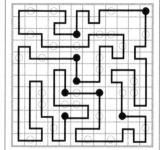

PAGE 116 **NONOGRAM 99**

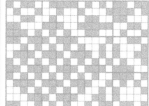

DESCRIPTION: CHECKERS

PAGE 117 **CALCUDOKU 100**

4	2	1	7	3	6	5
2	7	6	5	1	4	3
1	6	5	4	7	3	2
5	3	2	1	4	7	6
3	1	7	6	2	5	4
6	4	3	2	5	1	7
7	5	4	3	6	2	1

PAGE 118 **CRYPTIC PUZZLE 101**

Each name in the grid is connected to another name by a heart. Each pair of names traces out a letter, forming the five letters CUPID.

PAGE 119 **SUDOKU 102**

4	5	6	8	7	9	1	2	3
1	2	3	5	4	6	7	8	9
7	8	9	2	1	3	4	5	6
2	1	4	6	3	5	8	9	7
3	6	5	9	8	7	2	1	4
8	9	7	1	2	4	3	6	5
9	7	8	3	5	1	6	4	2
6	4	2	7	9	8	5	3	1
5	3	1	4	6	2	9	7	8

PAGE 120 **LOGIC GRID 103**

First place: Aiden, archery, pink, YAMM

Second place: Chloe, fencing, black, XYLO

Third place: Everett, biking, cyan, ZORO

Fourth place: Diego, footracing, gray, VENN

Last place: Beth, swimming, red, WILE

PAGE 122 **MASYU 104**

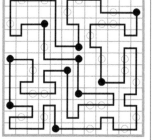

PAGE 123 **NONOGRAM 105**

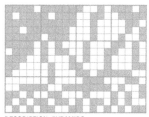

DESCRIPTION: PYRAMIDS

PAGE 124 **CALCUDOKU 106**

1	4	2	6	5	3	7
5	1	6	3	2	7	4
2	5	3	7	6	4	1
6	2	7	4	3	1	5
3	6	4	1	7	5	2
4	7	5	2	1	6	3
7	3	1	5	4	2	6

PAGE 125 **CRYPTIC PUZZLE 107**

There is a unique way to fill the three given words into the grid using Braille. Once done, the five shaded boxes give five Braille letters spelling CHILI.

PAGE 126 **LOGIC GRID 108**

Best ratings: Bravo, news, WRDE, Yankee

Second-best ratings: Charlie, game show, WQKG, Zulu

Middle-rated: Echo, talk show, WULV, Victor

Second-worst ratings: Alpha, comedy, WSBA, Whiskey

Worst ratings: Delta, drama, WTCC, X-ray

ANSWERS

PAGE 128 SUDOKU 109

6	3	5	1	2	4	7	8	9
1	2	4	9	8	7	5	3	6
9	8	7	6	3	5	4	2	1
5	4	6	2	1	3	9	7	8
2	1	3	8	7	9	6	4	5
8	7	9	5	4	6	3	1	2
3	5	1	7	9	8	2	6	4
4	6	2	3	5	1	8	9	7
7	9	8	4	6	2	1	5	3

PAGE 129 MASYU 110

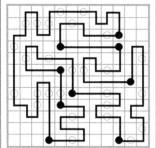

PAGE 130 NONOGRAM 111

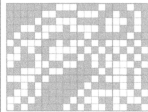

DESCRIPTION: BRIDE

PAGE 131 CALCUDOKU 112

5	3	2	4	1	6	7
3	1	7	2	6	4	5
1	6	5	7	4	2	3
7	5	4	6	3	1	2
2	7	6	1	5	3	4
6	4	3	5	2	7	1
4	2	1	3	7	5	6

PAGE 132 CRYPTIC PUZZLE 113

Each word should be filled into the grid of flowers according to its compass directions, beginning on a flower with four petals. Doing so spells BLOOM on the shaded flowers.

PAGE 133 SUDOKU 114

7	9	8	4	6	5	2	3	1
4	6	5	1	3	2	8	9	7
1	3	2	7	9	8	5	6	4
6	2	4	5	1	3	7	8	9
9	8	7	6	2	4	3	1	5
5	1	3	9	8	7	4	2	6
8	7	9	3	5	6	1	4	2
3	5	6	2	4	1	9	7	8
2	4	1	8	7	9	6	5	3

PAGE 134 MASYU 115

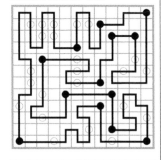

PAGE 135 NONOGRAM 116

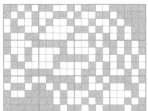

DESCRIPTION: TURTLE

PAGE 136 LOGIC GRID 117

ground floor: Emily, information technology, D, seven years,

first floor: Beth, accounting, C, three months,

second floor: Chris, supply chain management, B, four years,

third floor: Dean, marketing, E, two years,

fourth floor: Anna, human resources, A, a decade,

PAGE 138 CALCUDOKU 118

3	6	2	7	4	1	5
2	5	1	6	3	7	4
1	4	7	5	2	6	3
7	3	6	4	1	5	2
5	1	4	2	6	3	7
4	7	3	1	5	2	6
6	2	5	3	7	4	1

PAGE 139 CRYPTIC PUZZLE 119

Letting the vowels AEIOU be 1 and consonants be 0, each word gives a binary number, spelling USE MIDDLE LETTERS. The middle letters of the marked words spell REBOOT.

PAGE 140 SUDOKU 120

9	8	7	3	1	5	4	6	2
6	2	4	7	8	9	3	5	1
5	1	3	4	2	6	7	9	8
1	3	2	5	6	4	8	7	9
4	6	5	8	9	7	2	1	3
7	9	8	2	3	1	5	4	6
8	7	9	1	4	2	6	3	5
2	4	1	6	5	3	9	8	7
3	5	6	9	7	8	1	2	4

ANSWERS

PAGE 141 MASYU 121

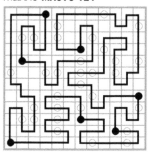

PAGE 142 NONOGRAM 122

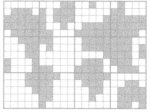

DESCRIPTION: ATLAS

PAGE 143 CALCUDOKU 123

3	7	5	1	4	6	2
5	2	7	3	6	1	4
1	5	3	6	2	4	7
6	3	1	4	7	2	5
2	6	4	7	3	5	1
4	1	6	2	5	7	3
7	4	2	5	1	3	6

PAGE 144 LOGIC GRID 124

A: Cindy, English, rap, Will

B: David, art, classic, Xander

C: Eric, science, jazz, Zelda

D: Bianca, history, metal, Violet

F: Adam, mathematics, electronic, Yvonne

PAGE 146 CRYPTIC PUZZLE 125

By placing letters in the chessboard so the names overlap correctly, the message NINE TWENTY NINETEEN... is revealed. Converting each number to a letter spells the solution ITS CHECKMATE.

PAGE 147 SUDOKU 126

8	9	7	4	5	6	3	1	2
2	3	1	7	8	9	6	4	5
5	6	4	1	2	3	9	7	8
7	8	9	6	4	2	1	5	3
4	2	6	5	3	1	8	9	7
3	1	5	9	7	8	2	6	4
6	5	3	2	1	4	7	8	9
9	7	8	3	6	5	4	2	1
1	4	2	8	9	7	5	3	6

PAGE 148 MASYU 127

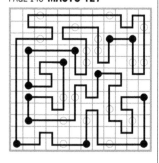

PAGE 149 NONOGRAM 128

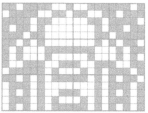

DESCRIPTION: TAJ MAHAL

PAGE 150 LOGIC GRID 129

100 gold: Darkeye, hook hand, violet, Tortuga

200 gold: Evilear, parrot, yellow, Orange Bay

300 gold: Arsonnose, eyepatch, brown, St. Mary's Island

400 gold: Blackbeard, cutlass, green, Port Royal

500 gold: Cursechin, treasure map, cerulean, New Providence

PAGE 152 CALCUDOKU 130

2	1	5	6	7	3	4
6	5	2	3	4	7	1
4	3	7	1	2	5	6
5	4	1	2	3	6	7
3	2	6	7	1	4	5
7	6	3	4	5	1	2
1	7	4	5	6	2	3

PAGE 153 CRYPTIC PUZZLE 131

Draw the path taken by the apprentice to the center of the maze. Using the letters found within adjacent connected groups of forbidden squares, the solution UNDERSTUDY may be spelled.

PAGE 154 SUDOKU 132

1	4	2	7	8	9	3	5	6
9	7	8	5	3	6	2	4	1
6	5	3	4	2	1	8	7	9
5	6	4	3	1	2	7	9	8
8	9	7	6	4	5	1	3	2
2	3	1	9	7	8	4	6	5
3	1	5	8	9	7	6	2	4
7	8	9	2	6	4	5	1	3
4	2	6	1	5	3	9	8	7

ANSWERS

PAGE 155 **MASYU 133**

PAGE 156 **NONOGRAM 134**

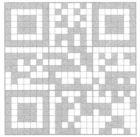

THIS IMAGE IS A QR CODE THAT CAN BE
READ WITH YOUR PHONE. GIVE IT A TRY!

PAGE 157 **CALCUDOKU 135**

8	1	5	2	4	7	3	6
4	5	1	6	8	3	7	2
6	7	3	8	2	5	1	4
5	6	2	7	1	4	8	3
2	3	7	4	6	1	5	8
3	4	8	5	7	2	6	1
7	8	4	1	3	6	2	5
1	2	6	3	5	8	4	7

PAGE 158 **LOGIC GRID 136**

First house: Diana, red, coffee, fox, lime

Second house: Bob, ivory, milk, zebra, peach

Middle house: Carl, blue, water, horse, tangerine

Fourth house: Eve, green, orange juice, dog, cherry

Last house: Alice, yellow, tea, snails, raspberry

PAGE 160 **CRYPTIC PUZZLE 137**

After the crisscross puzzle is filled with the solutions to the other 24 cryptic puzzles, look for where the three given letters in each square appear as the corners of a square in the crisscross. The fourth corners of each square spell the solution, FACTOR.

MORE PUZZLE FUN

Even if you've worked through every puzzle in this book, there's no reason the fun should stop here. Here are a few puzzle resources and communities you may be interested in learning more about.

PUZZLED PINT

PuzzledPint.com

Puzzled Pint is a casual puzzle-solving event for adults held at bars and pubs in more than 60 cities across the world. On the second Tuesday of every month, you can grab a couple friends and solve a free themed set of four cryptic puzzles and a metapuzzle alongside (or against!) a community of like-minded puzzlers.

DASH—DIFFERENT AREA SAME HUNT

PlayDASH.org

DASH takes fun puzzle-solving to the streets of more than 20 cities across the world. Teams of three to five solvers are challenged with a series of cryptic puzzles. Many puzzles aren't just on paper: You might need to build a three-dimensional jigsaw puzzle or inspect a suspicious deck of marked cards to solve the overarching mystery of each game.

MATHEMATICAL PUZZLE PROGRAMS

MaPPMath.org

The mission of Mathematical Puzzle Programs (MaPP) is to organize quality events that get students having fun by learning and using mathematics. If you know a 7th- to 12th-grade student who'd love to learn math by way of puzzles, check MaPP's website to see if it has partnered with a college campus near you.

PUZZLE HUNT CALENDAR

PuzzleHuntCalendar.com

There are plenty more puzzle events, both in person and online. The Puzzle Hunt Calendar is the best place to see what's coming up.

ROOM ESCAPE ARTIST

RoomEscapeArtist.com

If you're looking for a short immersive puzzle experience, you should try a local escape room—if you haven't already! There are a number of resources out there to see what's worth your time and money, but I personally follow David and Lisa at *Room Escape Artist*, who do a great job reviewing all sorts of puzzle experiences around the world.

ACKNOWLEDGMENTS

Quick shout-outs are due to several people who supported me in the preparation of this book: Thanks to Andrea Blumberg, Bryan Clair, Phillip Clontz, Tracy Cobbs, Jenn Dumont, Julie Gaddy, Steve Gaddy, Eric Harshbarger, Charles McPillan, Erin McPillan, Trent Webb, and especially my wife Jessica and daughter Madeline.

"Love Connection" (page 118) is adapted from a puzzle by Jennifer Dumont. Twitter: @JenoftheMT

"Compass Rose" (page 132) is adapted from a puzzle by Andrea Blumberg. Website: AndreaBlumberg.com

"Electronic Mail" (page 139) is adapted from a puzzle by Eric Harshbarger. Website: EricHarshbarger.com

"The Puzzler's Apprentice" (page 153) is adapted from a puzzle by Bryan Clair. Twitter: @TurtleGraphics

ABOUT THE AUTHOR

Steven Clontz is a mathematician, professor, and puzzle designer living in Mobile, Alabama, with his wife Jessica and daughter Madeline. Dr. Clontz graduated with his PhD in mathematics from Auburn University, specializing in game theory and topology. His puzzles and games have been featured by the National Museum of Mathematics and the international puzzle events DASH and Puzzled Pint. He also serves as director of Mathematical Puzzle Programs, which has designed and organized puzzle events at college campuses and math camps around the world. As an educator, Dr. Clontz uses active learning techniques such as team-based inquiry learning to allow his students to discover mathematics for themselves by way of carefully scaffolded activities and puzzles.

Find him on the web at Clontz.org and on Twitter at @StevenXClontz.

CPSIA information can be obtained
at www.ICGtesting.com
Printed in the USA
BVHW061123250620
582268BV00002B/2

9 781646 111459